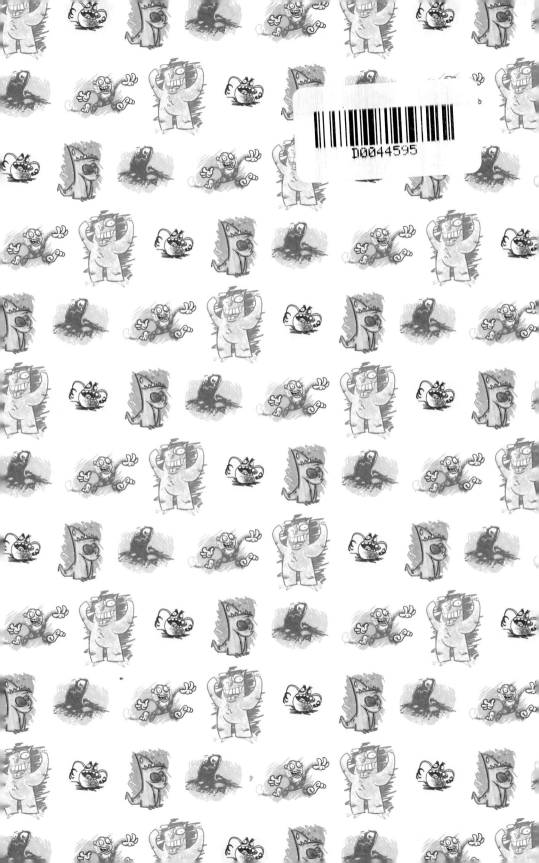

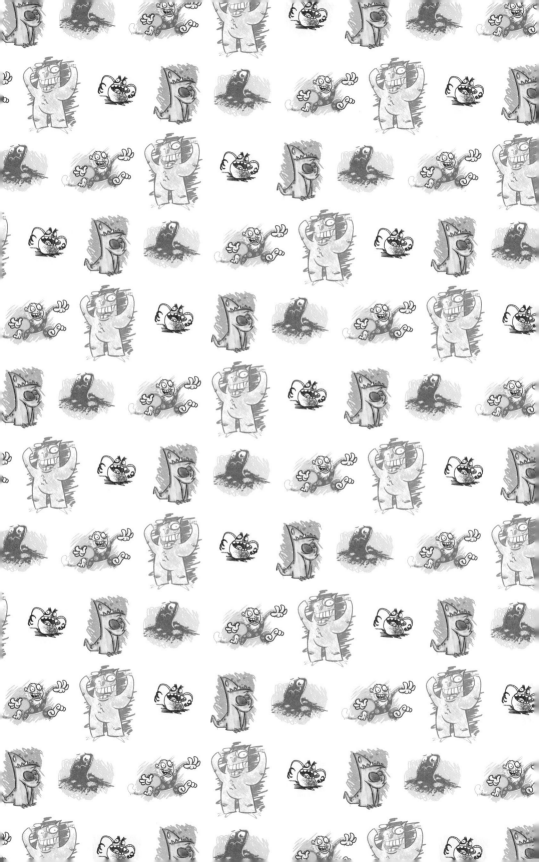

SKETCH MONSTERS

ESCAPE OF THE SCRIBBLES

by

JOSHUA WILLIAMSON

&

VINNY NAVARRETE

logo design by
VINNY NAVARRETE

book design by
KEITH WOOD

edited by
JILL BEATON

FOR MY MOM, DAD, FAMILY, AND FRIENDS WHO HAVE BEEN A HUGE HELP IN CONTINUING MY DREAM OF WRITING COMICS, ESPECIALLY JASON HO, THE BEST MOTIVATIONAL SPEAKER. OF COURSE, I HAVE TO THANK VINNY FOR BUSTING HIS BUTT TO GET THIS BOOK DONE, EVEN IF IT ALMOST MADE HIM GO BALD. THE BIGGEST THANKS GO TO MY WIFE WHO PUTS UP WITH HER RECLUSE HUSBAND. YOU'RE THE BEST, BABE.

—JOSH

I WOULD LIKE TO DEDICATE THIS BOOK TO KIDS OF ALL AGES AROUND THE WORLD, WHO LOVE COLORING AND MAKING STUFF.

—VINNY

ONI PRESS, INC.

PUBLISHER JOE NOZEMACK   EDITOR IN CHIEF JAMES LUCAS JONES

MARKETING DIRECTOR CORY CASONI   ART DIRECTOR KEITH WOOD   OPERATIONS DIRECTOR GEORGE ROHAC

EDITOR JILL BEATON   EDITOR CHARLIE CHU   PRODUCTION ASSISTANT DOUGLAS E. SHERWOOD

onipress.com • thejoshuawilliamson.com • vinnyville.carbonmade.com

Oni Press, Inc.
1305 SE M.L.K. Jr. Blvd.
Suite A
Portland, OR 97214
USA

First edition: October 2011

ISBN 978-1-934964-69-9

Library of Congress Control Number: 2011906144

1 3 5 7 9 10 8 6 4 2

Printed by TWP America, Inc. in Singapore, Singapore.

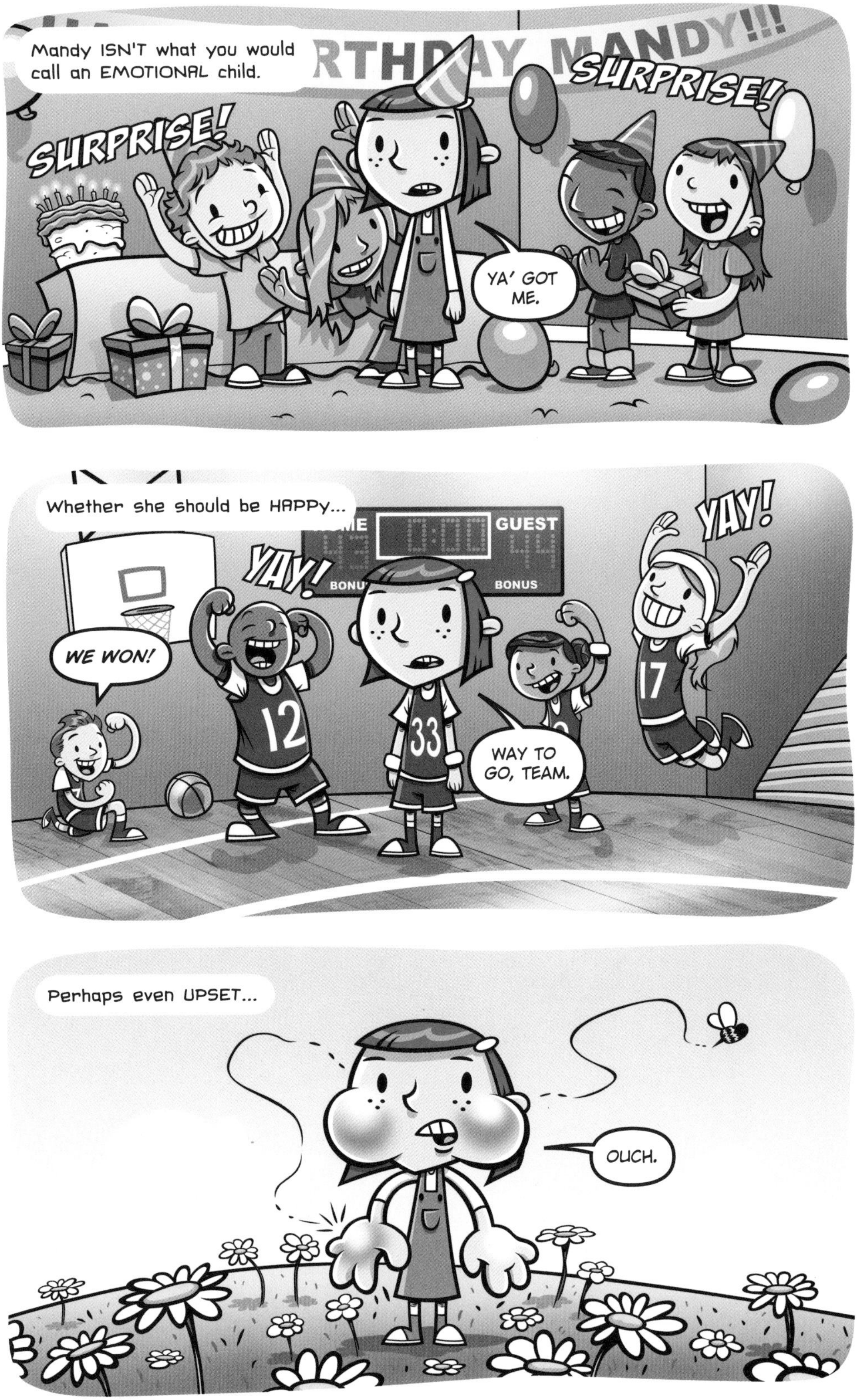

Mandy ISN'T what you would call an EMOTIONAL child.
SURPRISE!
SURPRISE!
YA' GOT ME.
Whether she should be HAPPY...
GUEST
BONUS
BONUS
YAY!
YAY!
WE WON!
WAY TO GO, TEAM.
Perhaps even UPSET...
OUCH.

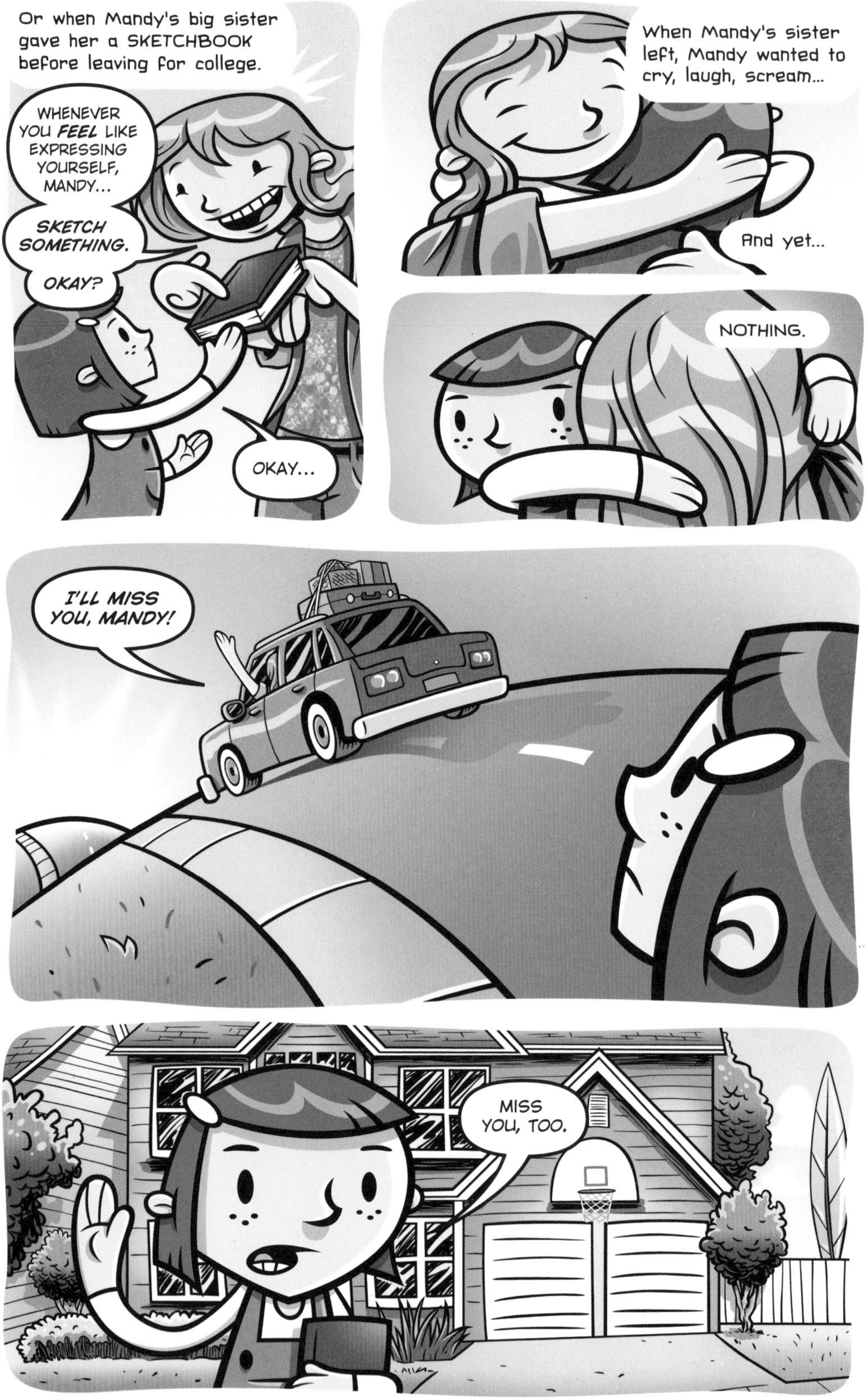

Or when Mandy's big sister gave her a SKETCHBOOK before leaving for college.
WHENEVER YOU FEEL LIKE EXPRESSING YOURSELF, MANDY...
SKETCH SOMETHING.
OKAY?
OKAY...
When Mandy's sister left, Mandy wanted to cry, laugh, scream...
And yet...
NOTHING.
I'LL MISS YOU, MANDY!
MISS YOU, TOO.

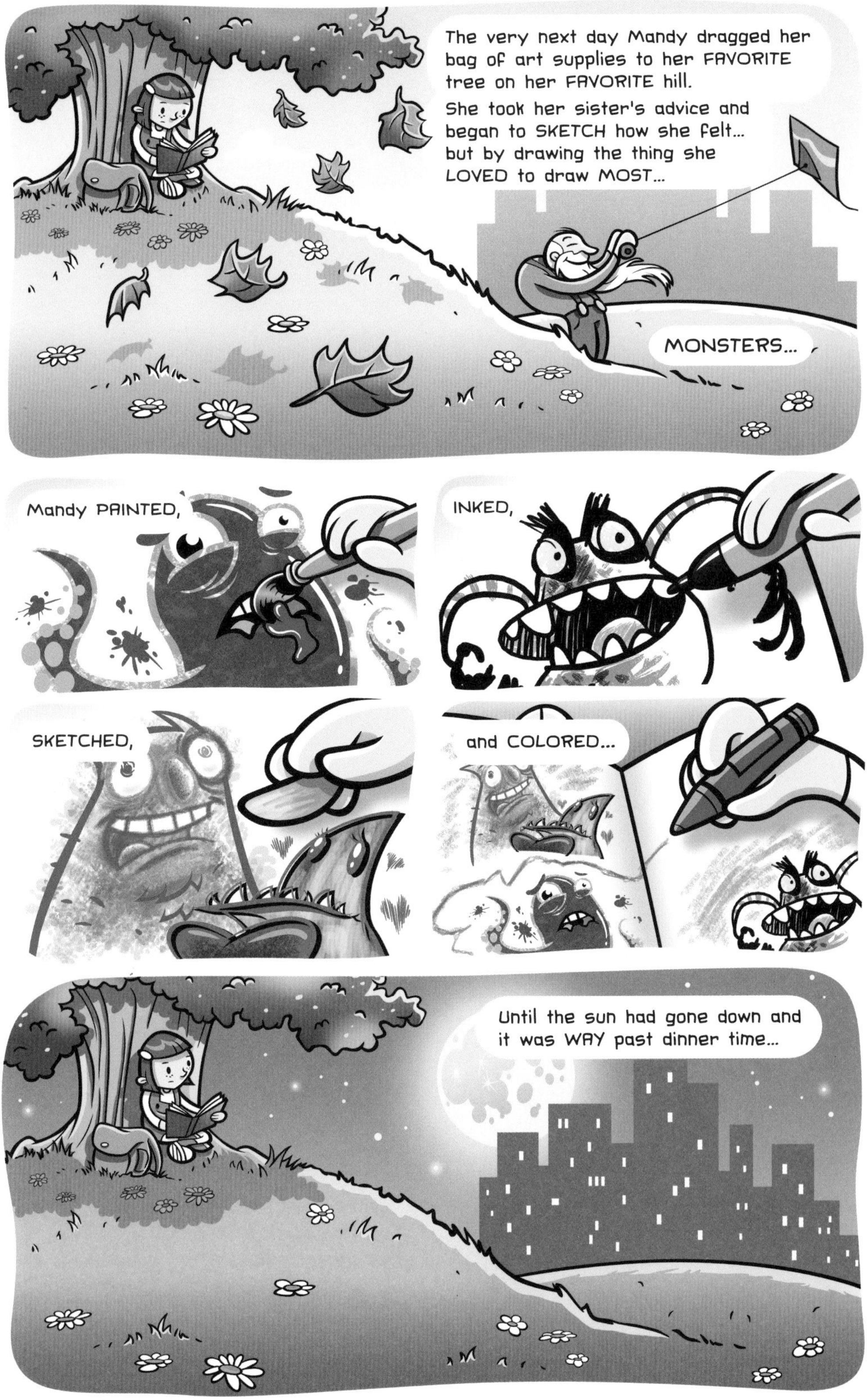
The very next day Mandy dragged her bag of art supplies to her FAVORITE tree on her FAVORITE hill.
She took her sister's advice and began to SKETCH how she felt... but by drawing the thing she LOVED to draw MOST...
MONSTERS...
Mandy PAINTED,
INKED,
SKETCHED,
and COLORED...
Until the sun had gone down and it was WAY past dinner time...

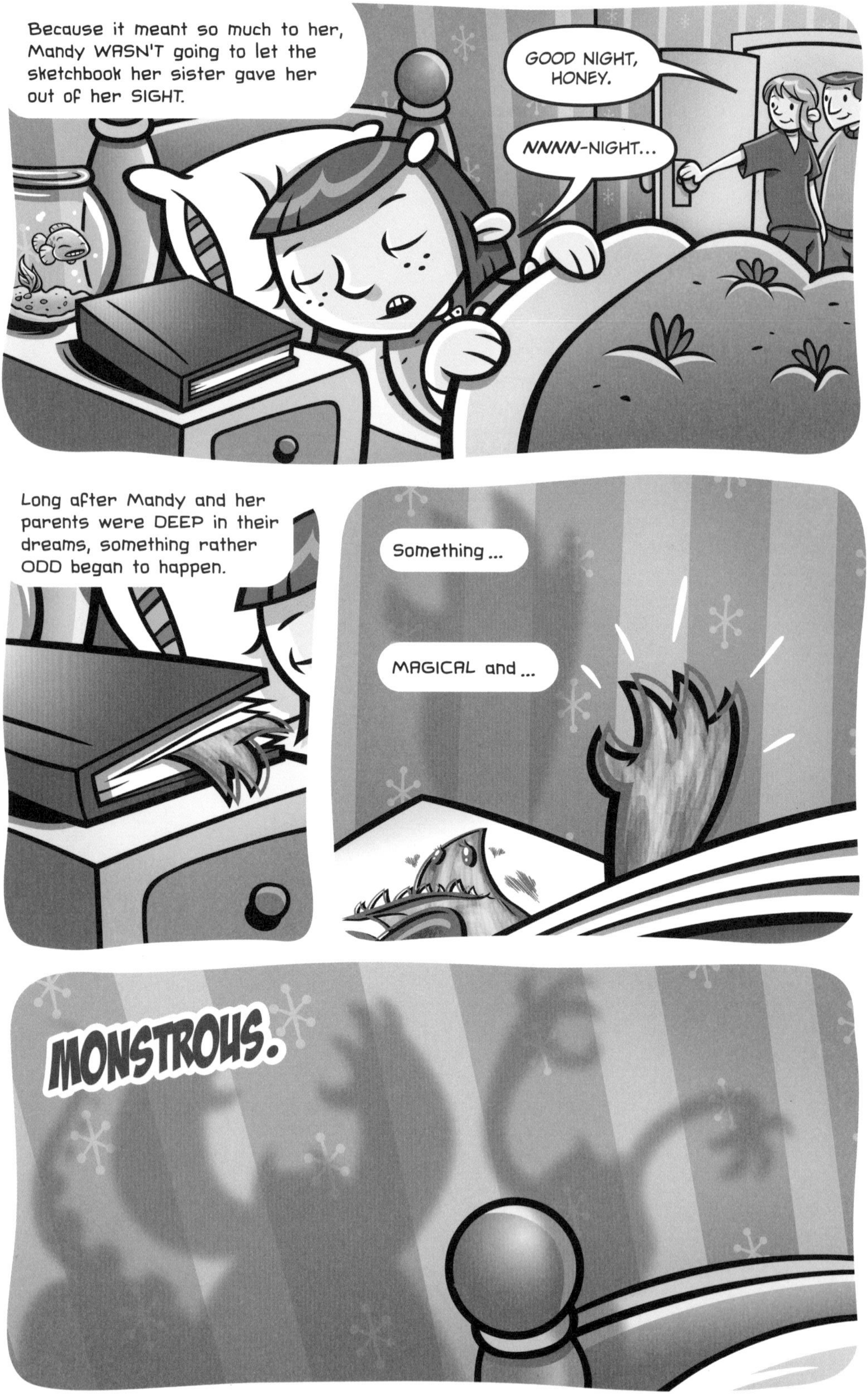
Because it meant so much to her, Mandy WASN'T going to let the sketchbook her sister gave her out of her SIGHT.
GOOD NIGHT, HONEY.
NNNN-NIGHT...
Long after Mandy and her parents were DEEP in their dreams, something rather ODD began to happen.
Something ...
MAGICAL and ...
MONSTROUS.

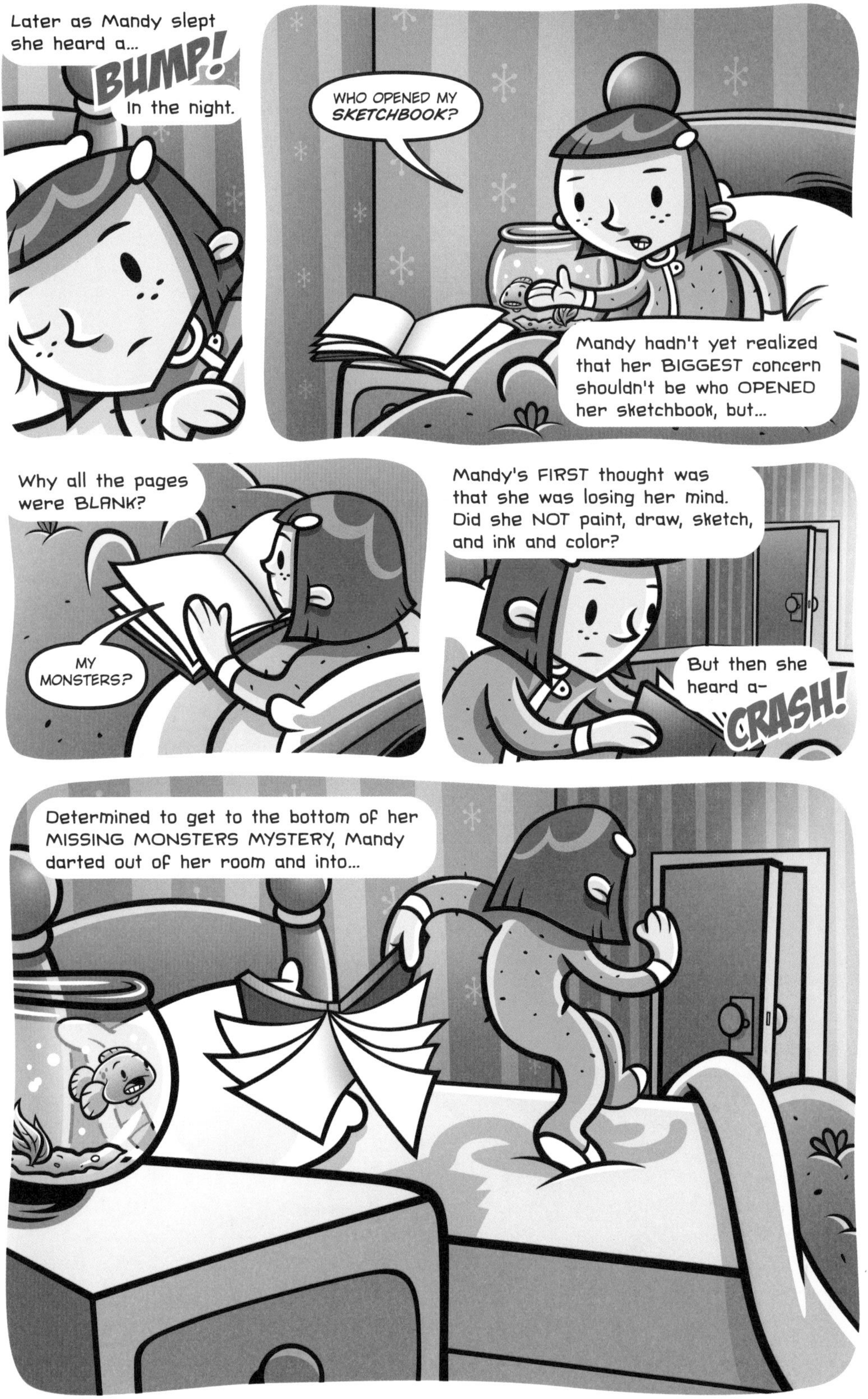
Later as Mandy slept she heard a...
BUMP!
In the night.
WHO OPENED MY SKETCHBOOK?
Mandy hadn't yet realized that her BIGGEST concern shouldn't be who OPENED her sketchbook, but...
Why all the pages were BLANK?
MY MONSTERS?
Mandy's FIRST thought was that she was losing her mind. Did she NOT paint, draw, sketch, and ink and color?
But then she heard a-
CRASH!
Determined to get to the bottom of her MISSING MONSTERS MYSTERY, Mandy darted out of her room and into...

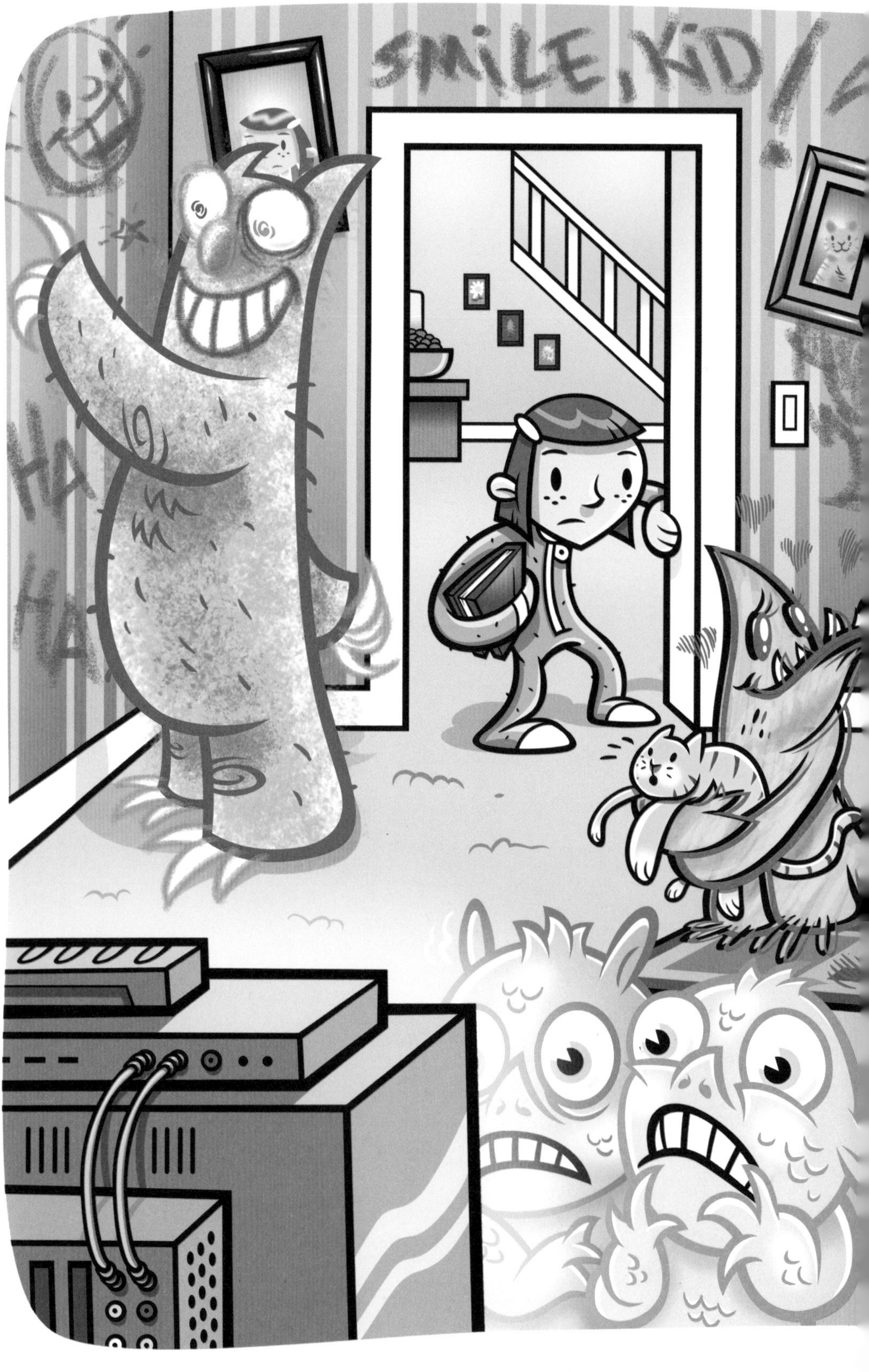
SMILE, KID!
HA
HA
HA

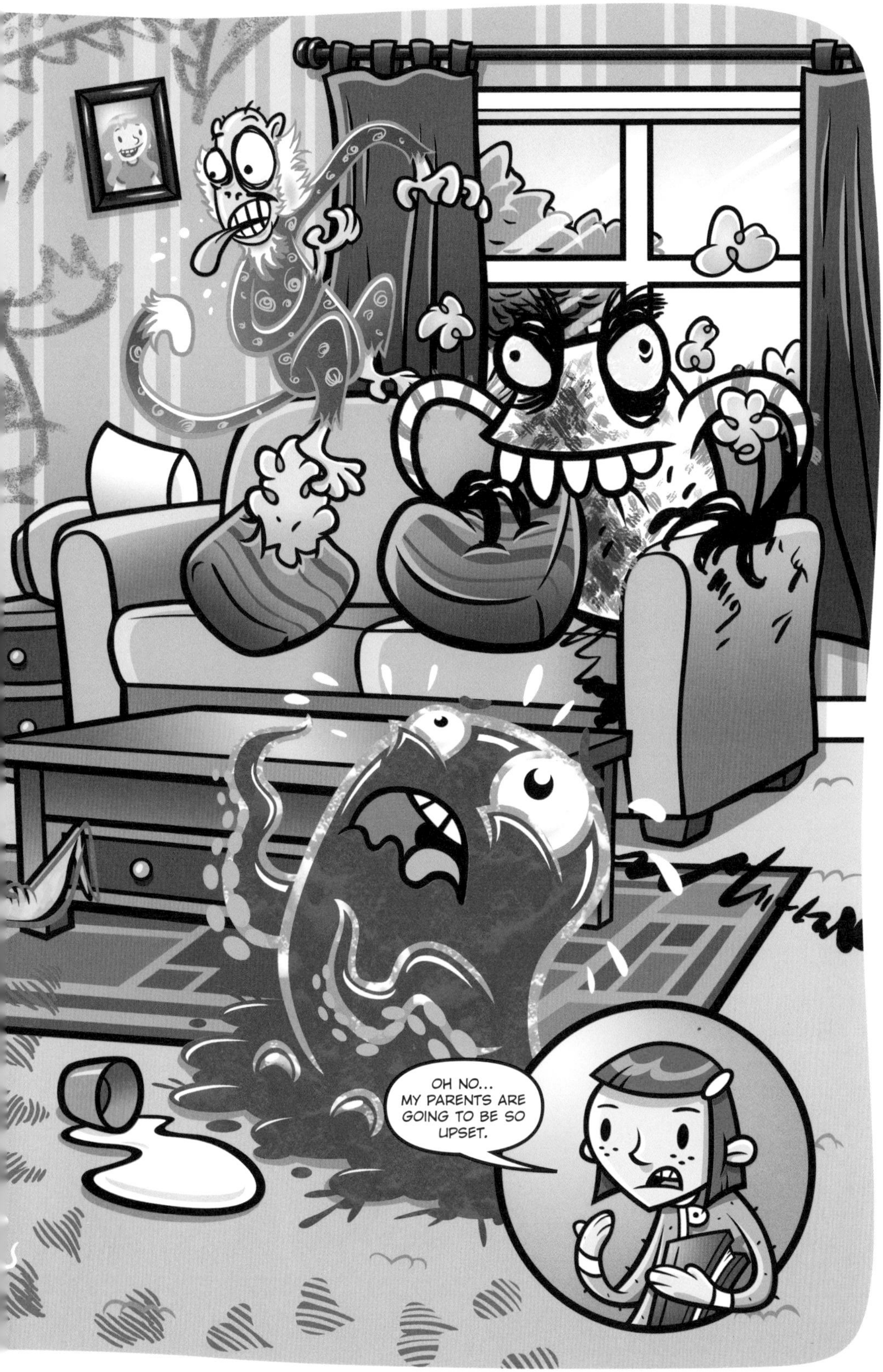
OH NO... MY PARENTS ARE GOING TO BE SO UPSET.

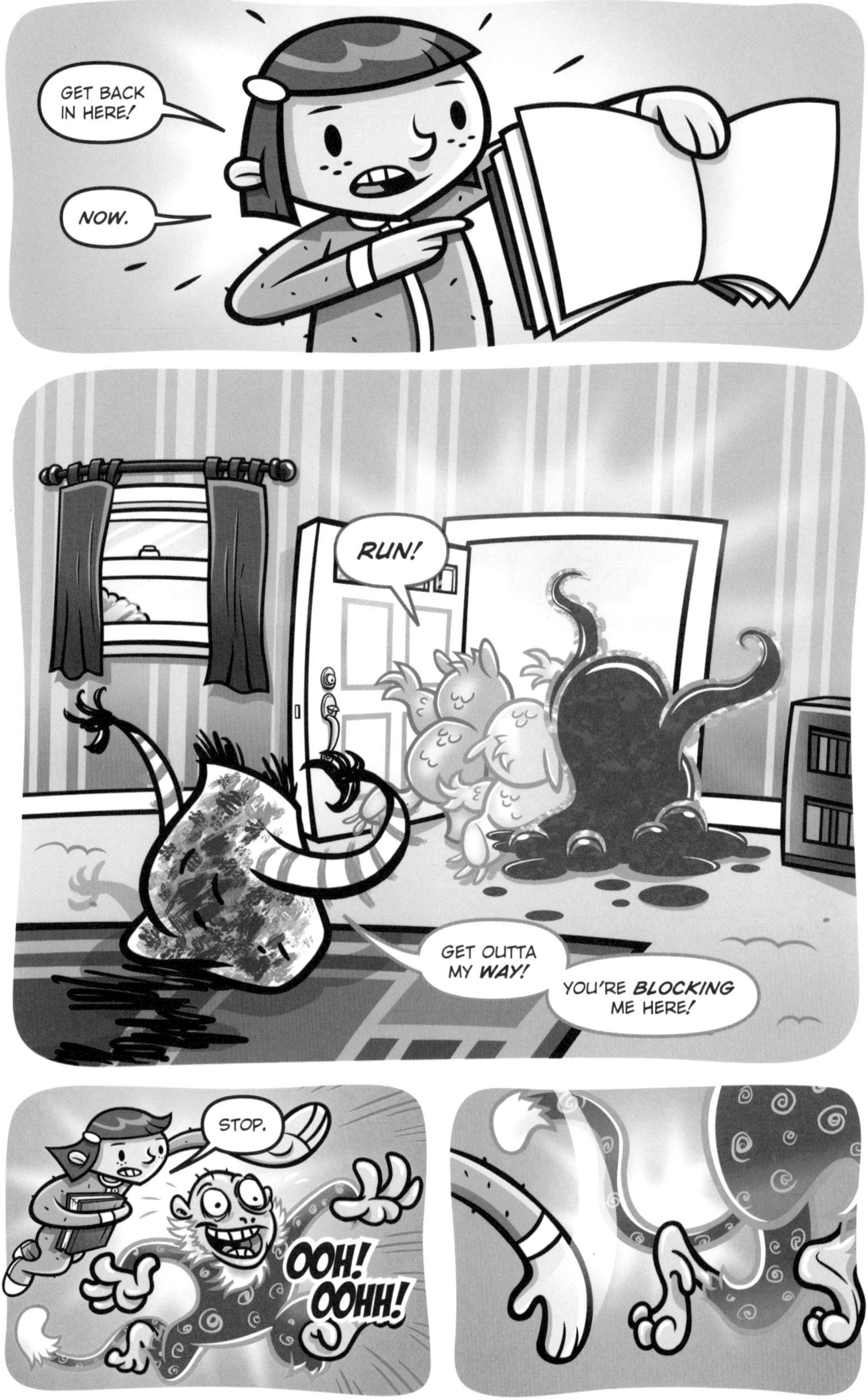
GET BACK IN HERE!
NOW.
RUN!
GET OUTTA MY WAY!
YOU'RE BLOCKING ME HERE!
STOP.
OOH! OOHH!

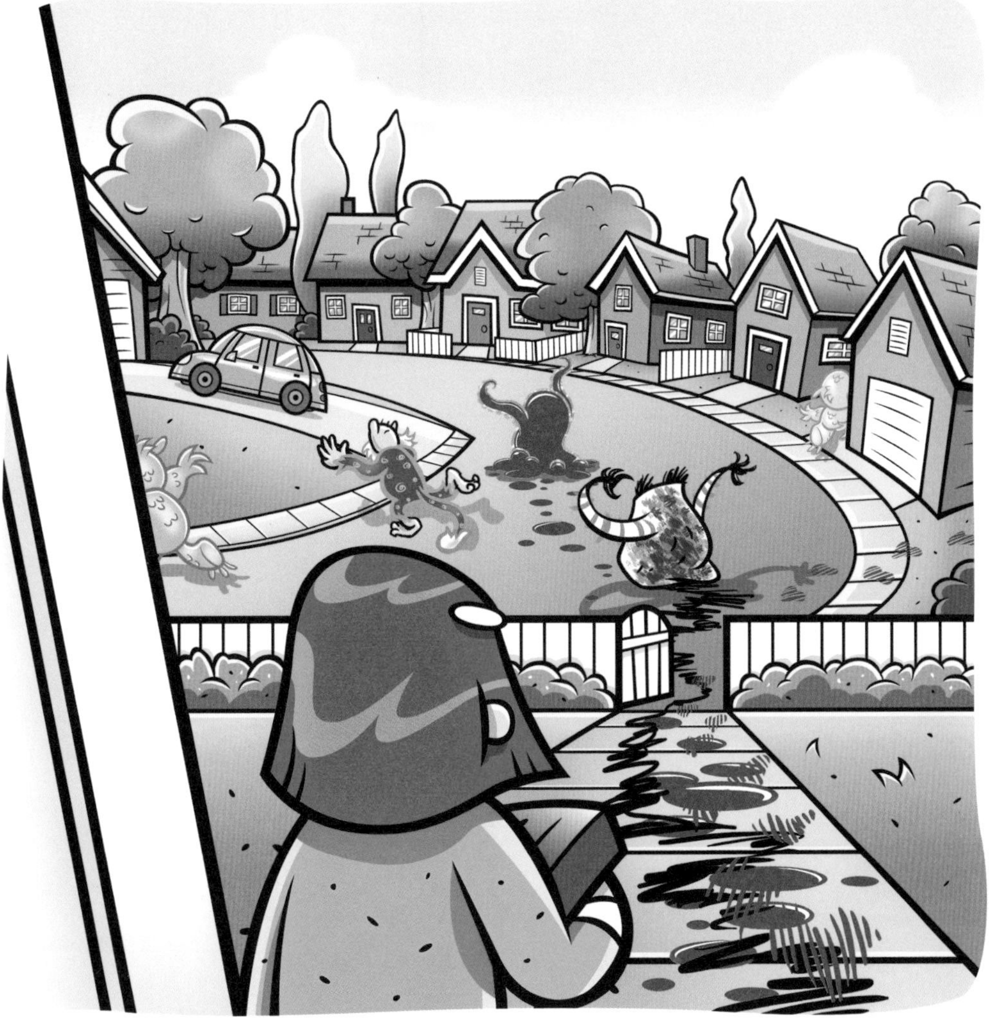

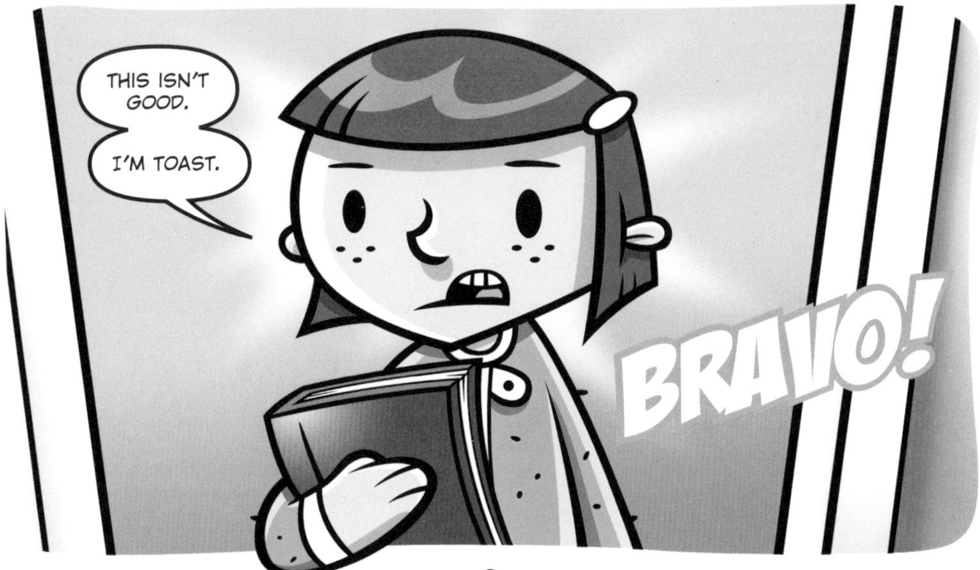
THIS ISN'T GOOD.
I'M TOAST.
BRAVO!

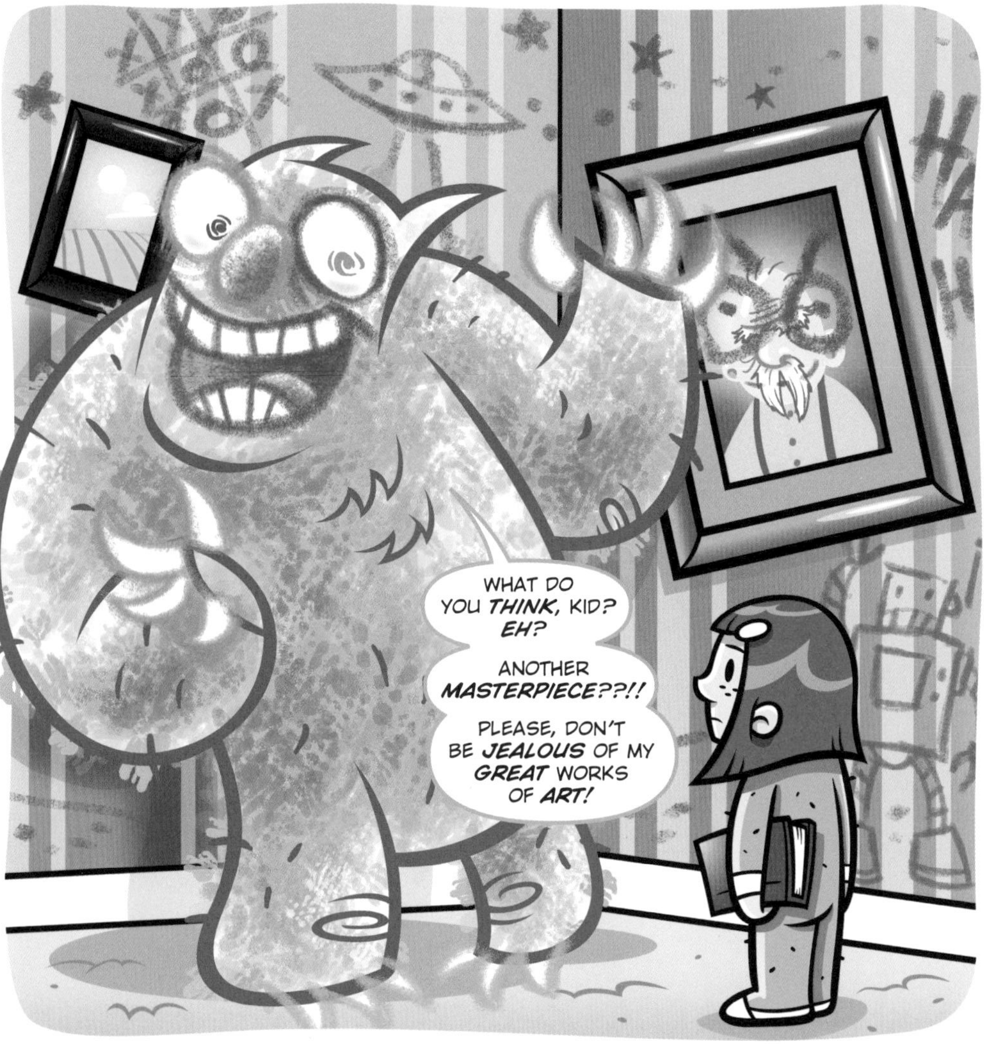
WHAT DO YOU THINK, KID? EH?
ANOTHER MASTERPIECE??!!
PLEASE, DON'T BE JEALOUS OF MY GREAT WORKS OF ART!

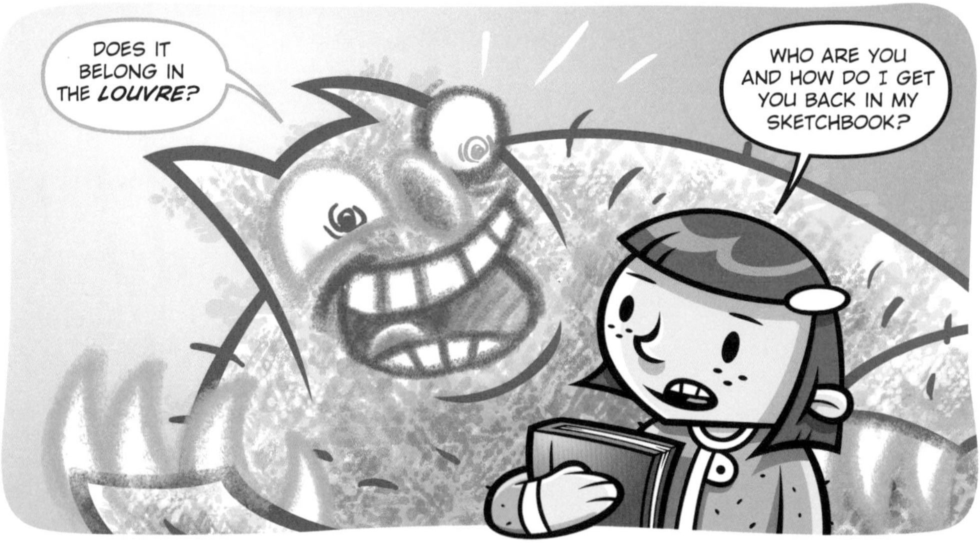
DOES IT BELONG IN THE LOUVRE?
WHO ARE YOU AND HOW DO I GET YOU BACK IN MY SKETCHBOOK?

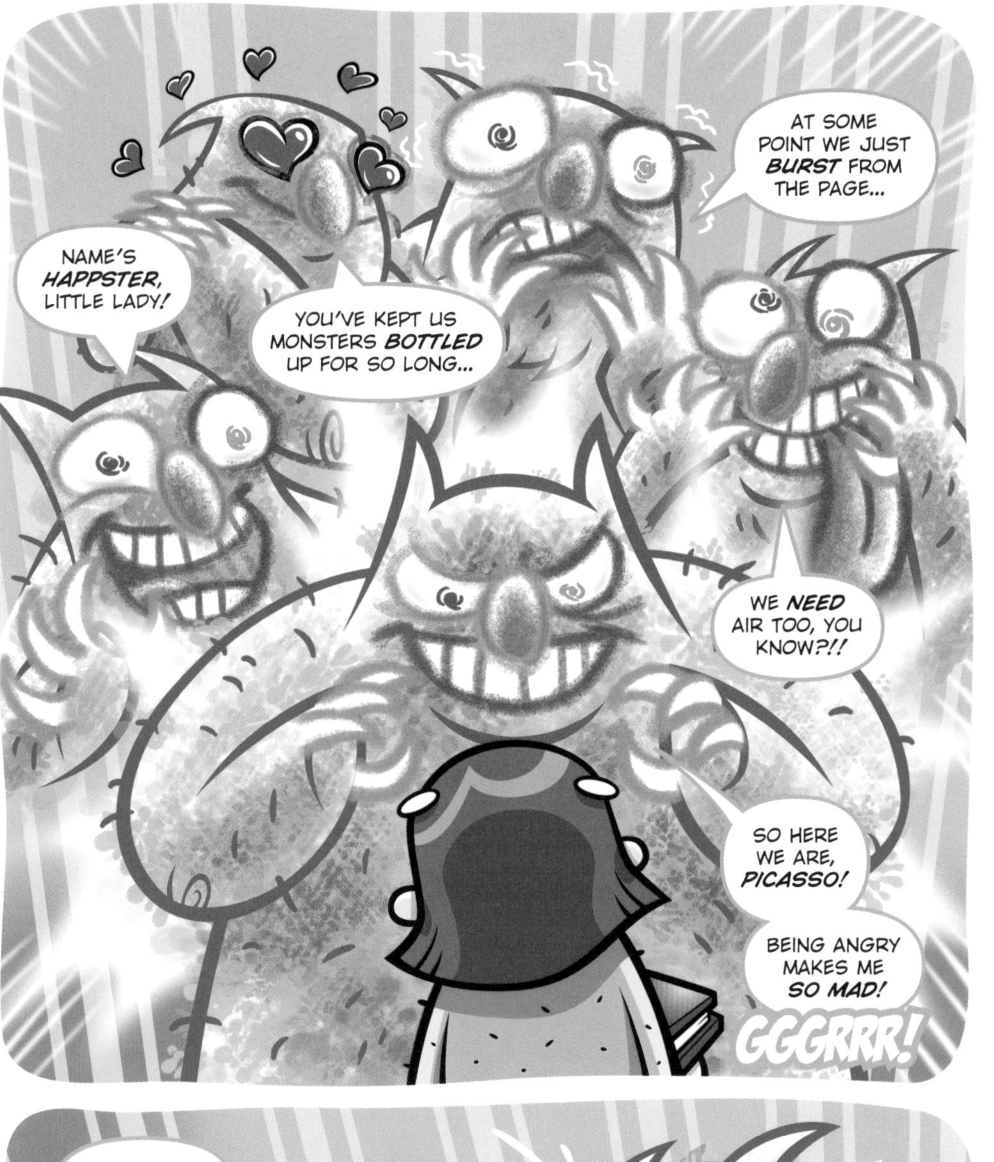
NAME'S *HAPPSTER*, LITTLE LADY!
YOU'VE KEPT US MONSTERS *BOTTLED* UP FOR SO LONG...
AT SOME POINT WE JUST *BURST* FROM THE PAGE...
WE *NEED* AIR TOO, YOU KNOW?!!
SO HERE WE ARE, *PICASSO!*
BEING ANGRY MAKES ME *SO MAD!*
GGGRRR!

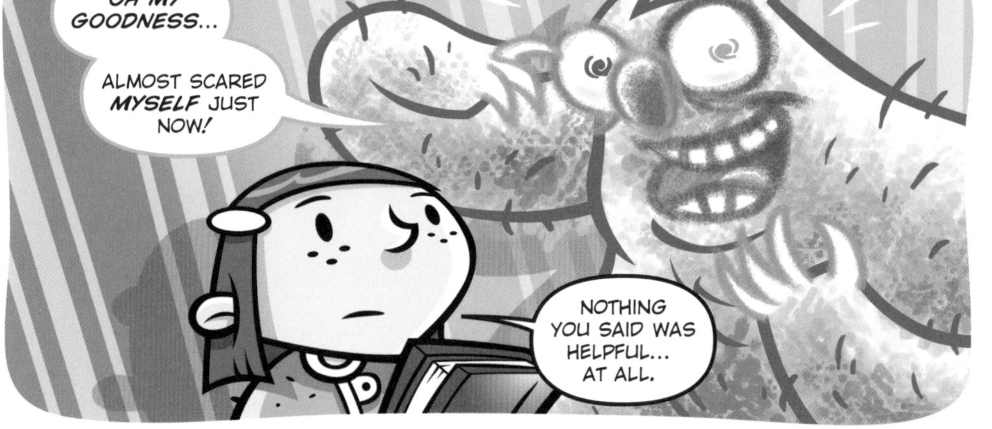
OH MY GOODNESS...
ALMOST SCARED *MYSELF* JUST NOW!
NOTHING YOU SAID WAS HELPFUL... AT ALL.

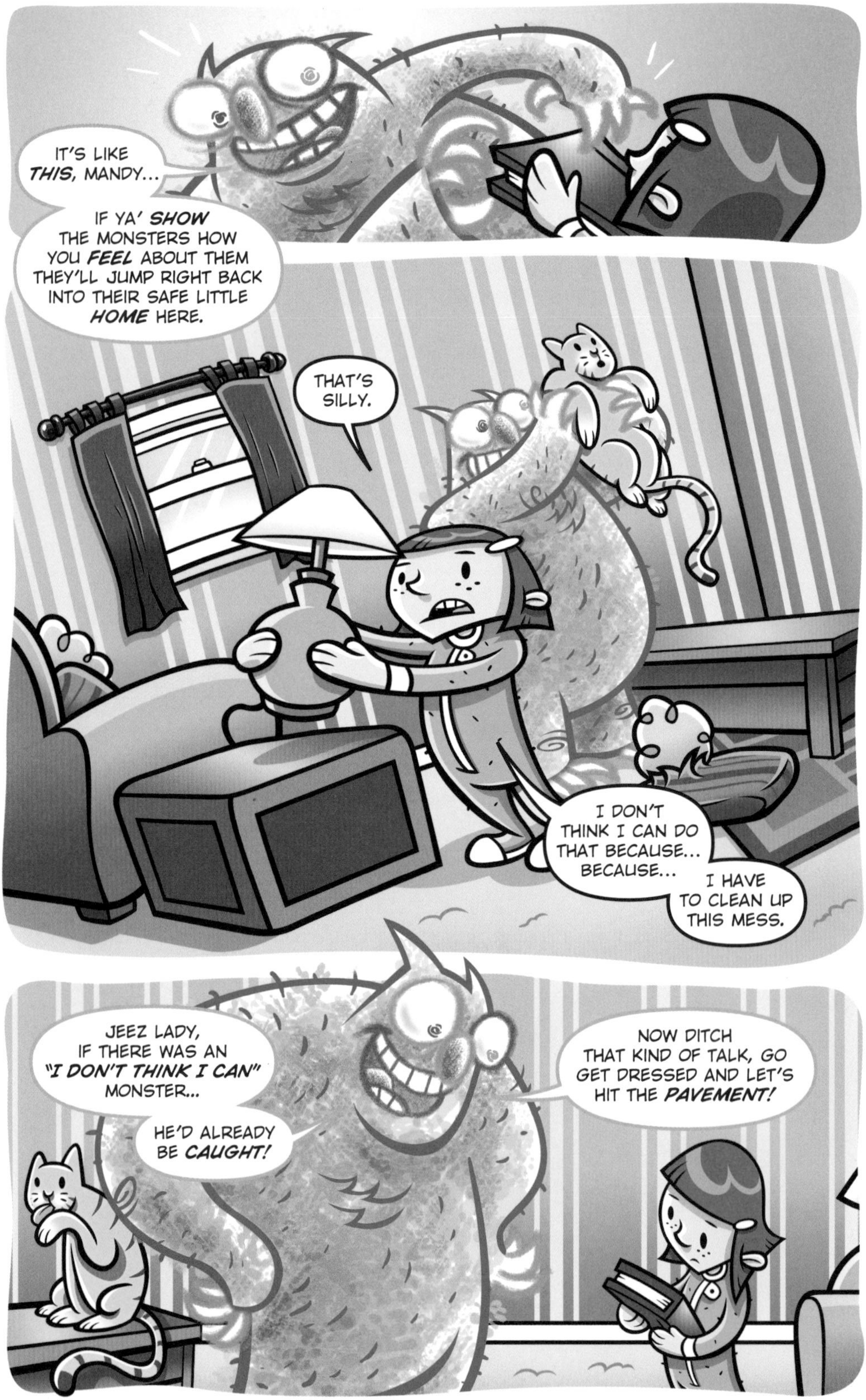
IT'S LIKE *THIS*, MANDY...
IF YA' *SHOW* THE MONSTERS HOW YOU *FEEL* ABOUT THEM THEY'LL JUMP RIGHT BACK INTO THEIR SAFE LITTLE *HOME* HERE.
THAT'S SILLY.
I DON'T THINK I CAN DO THAT BECAUSE... BECAUSE...
I HAVE TO CLEAN UP THIS MESS.
JEEZ LADY, IF THERE WAS AN *"I DON'T THINK I CAN"* MONSTER...
HE'D ALREADY BE *CAUGHT!*
NOW DITCH THAT KIND OF TALK, GO GET DRESSED AND LET'S HIT THE *PAVEMENT!*

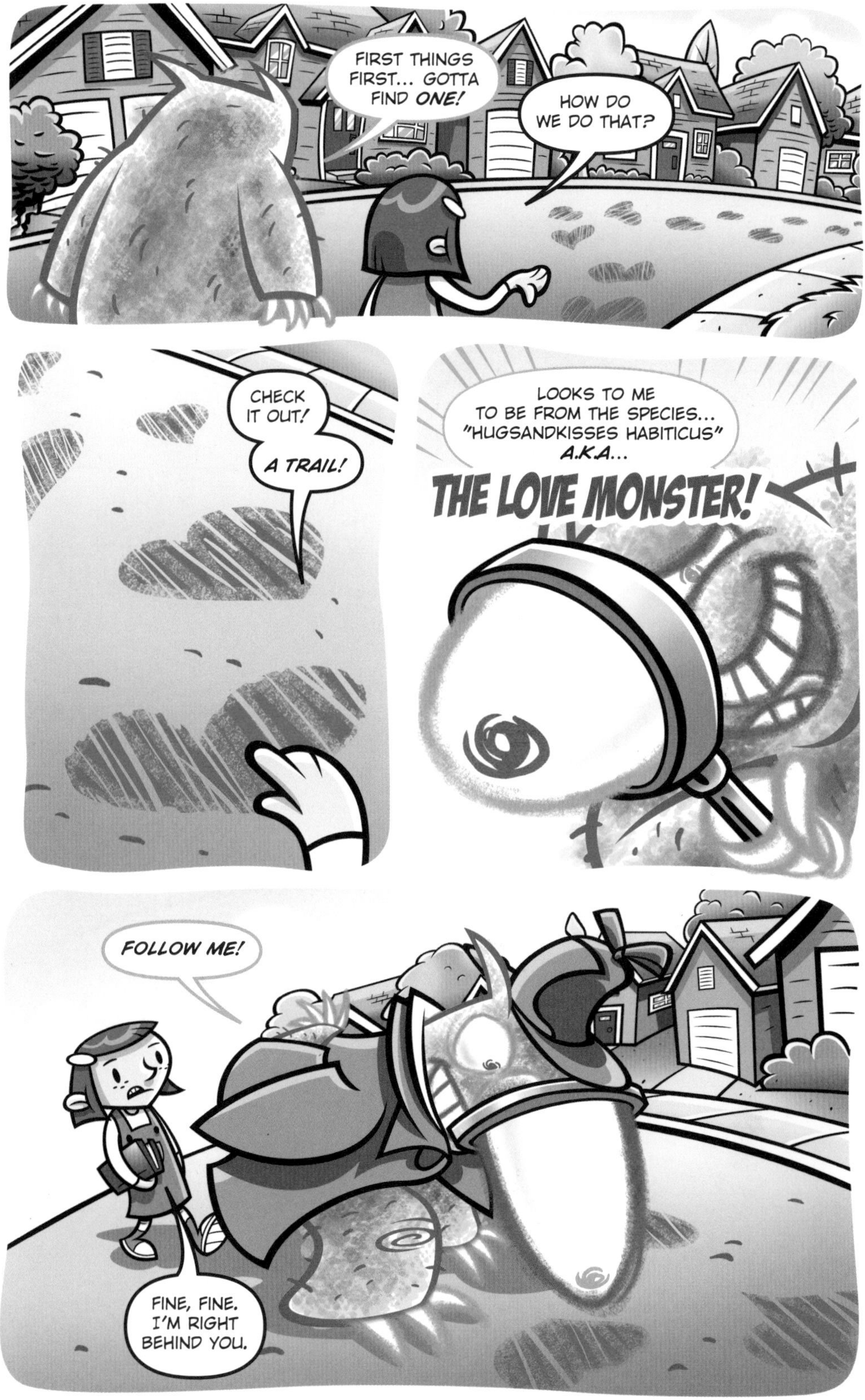
FIRST THINGS FIRST... GOTTA FIND ONE!
HOW DO WE DO THAT?
CHECK IT OUT!
A TRAIL!
LOOKS TO ME TO BE FROM THE SPECIES... "HUGSANDKISSES HABITICUS" A.K.A...
THE LOVE MONSTER!
FOLLOW ME!
FINE, FINE. I'M RIGHT BEHIND YOU.

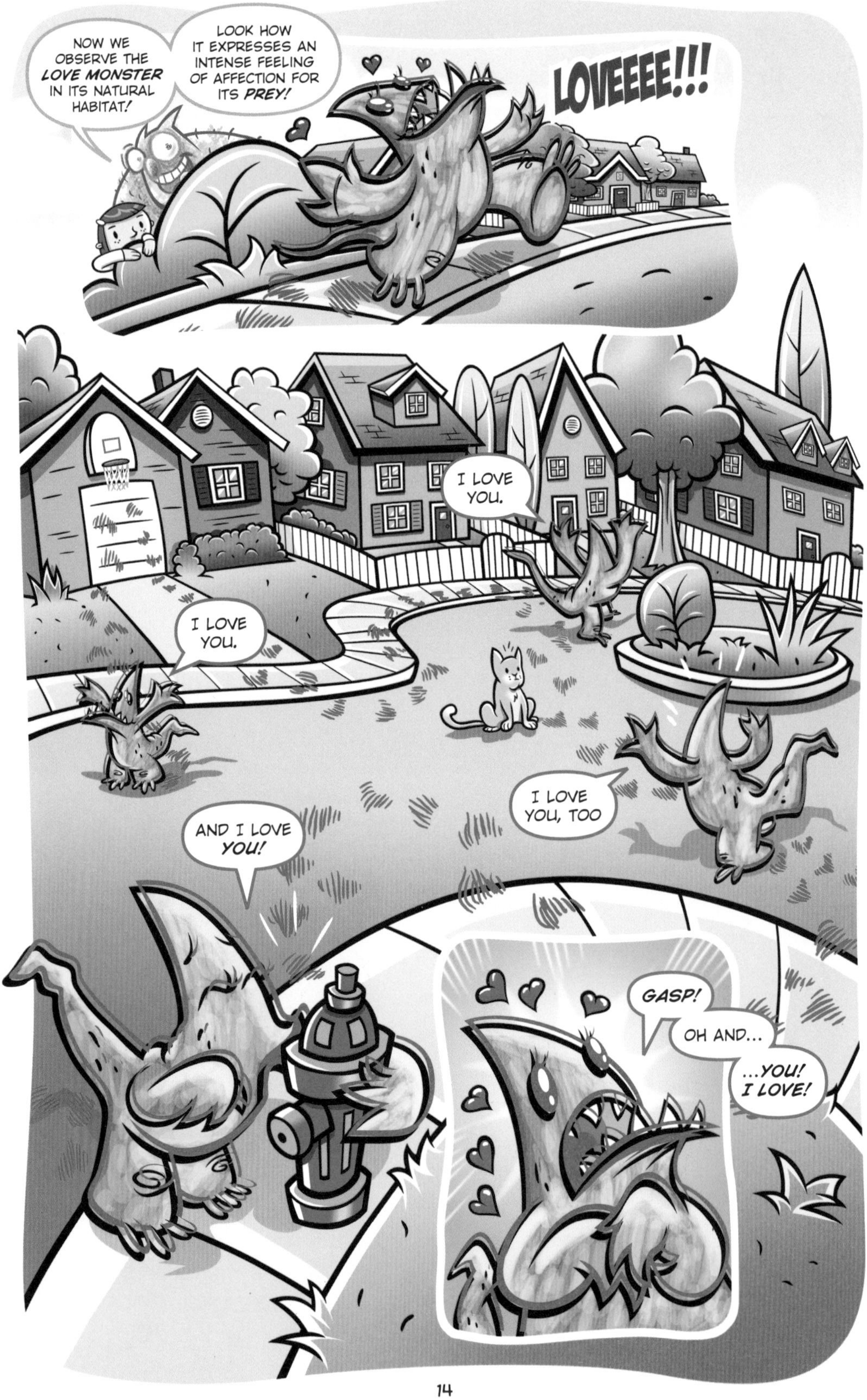
NOW WE OBSERVE THE *LOVE MONSTER* IN ITS NATURAL HABITAT!
LOOK HOW IT EXPRESSES AN INTENSE FEELING OF AFFECTION FOR ITS *PREY!*
LOVEEEE!!!
I LOVE YOU.
I LOVE YOU.
I LOVE YOU, TOO
AND I LOVE *YOU!*
GASP!
OH AND...
...YOU! I LOVE!

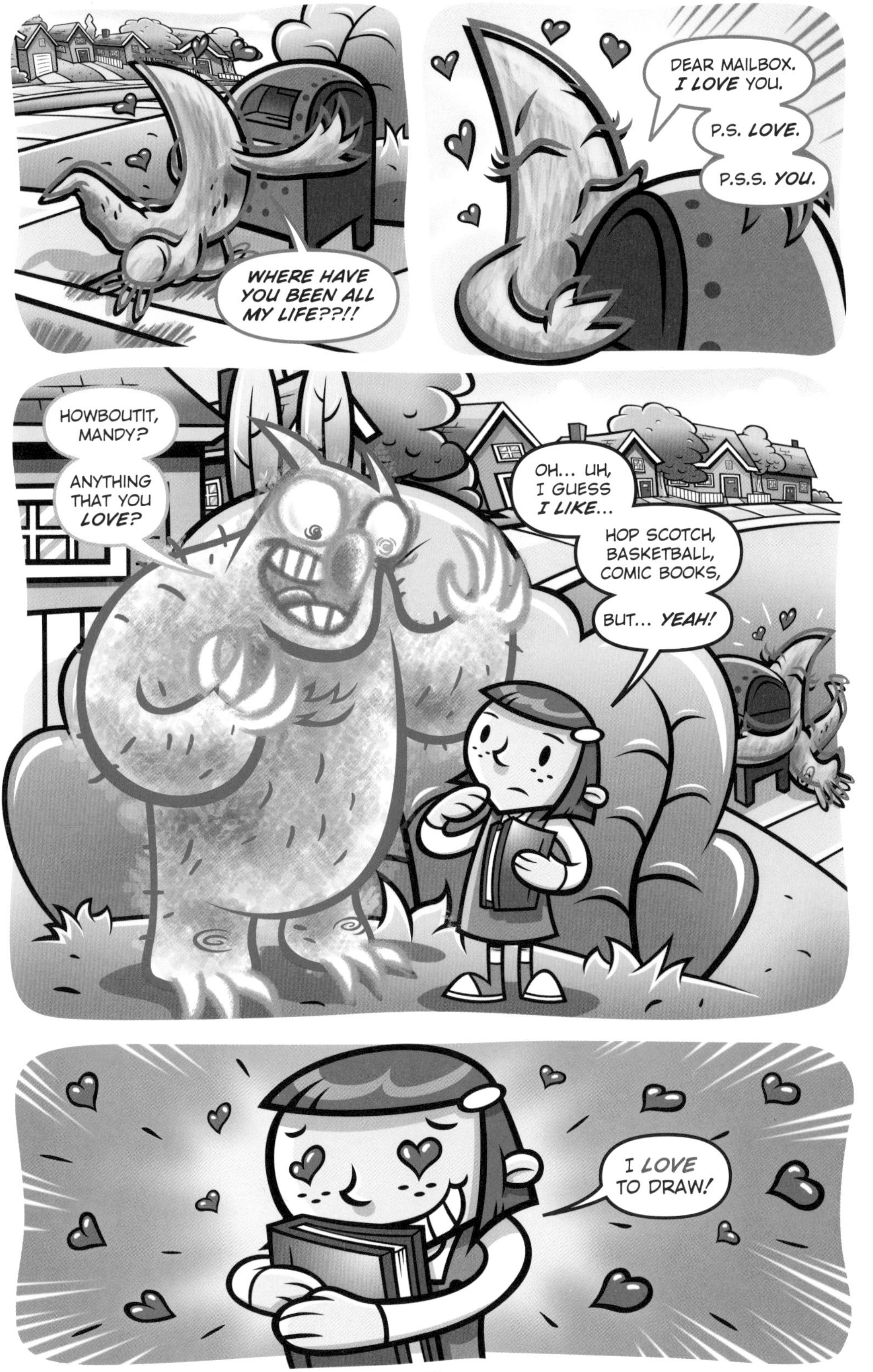
WHERE HAVE YOU BEEN ALL MY LIFE??!!
DEAR MAILBOX. I LOVE YOU.
P.S. LOVE.
P.S.S. YOU.
HOWBOUTIT, MANDY?
ANYTHING THAT YOU LOVE?
OH... UH, I GUESS I LIKE...
HOP SCOTCH, BASKETBALL, COMIC BOOKS,
BUT... YEAH!
I LOVE TO DRAW!

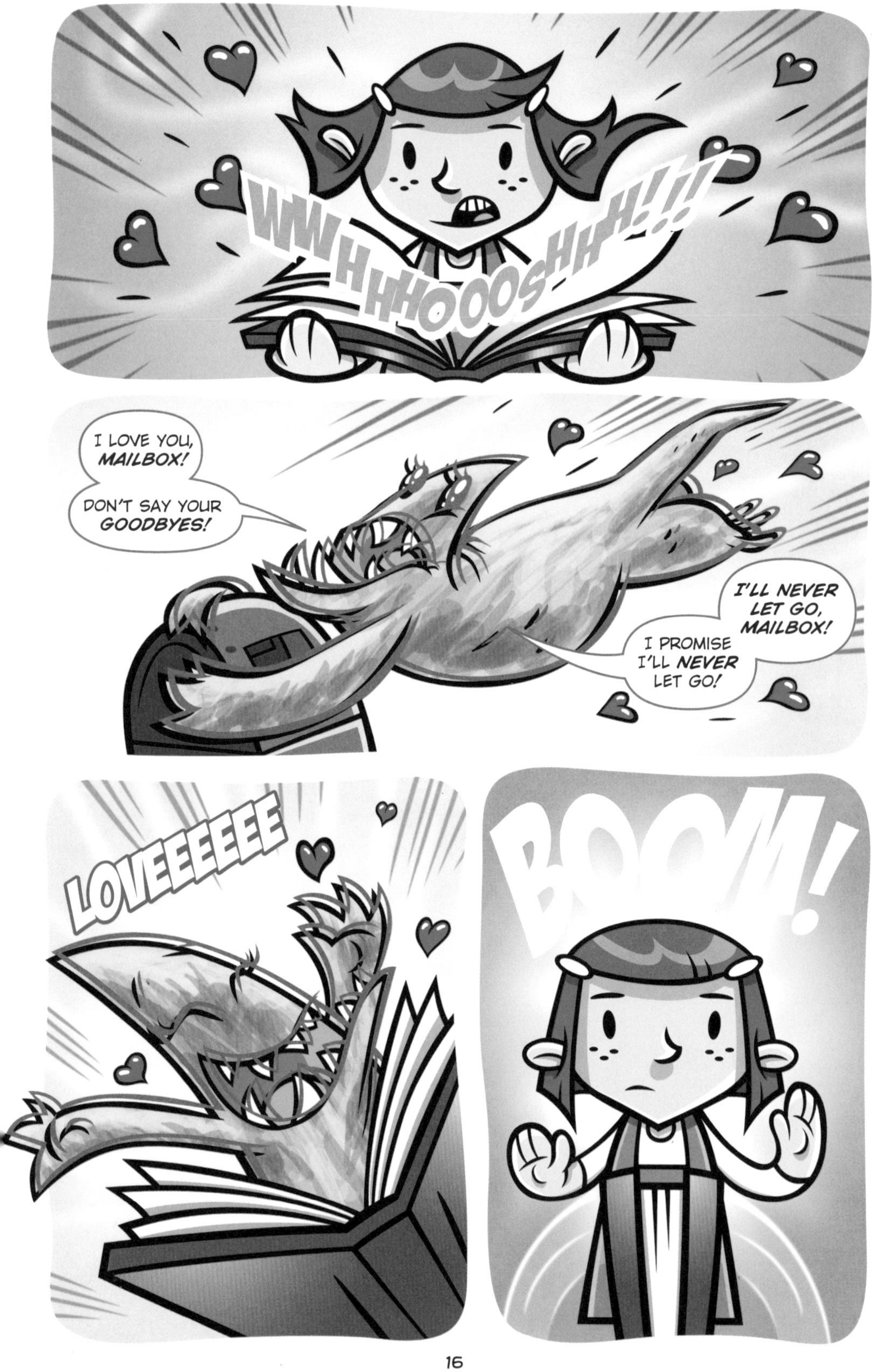
WWHHHOOOSHHH!!!
I LOVE YOU, MAILBOX!
DON'T SAY YOUR GOODBYES!
I'LL NEVER LET GO, MAILBOX!
I PROMISE I'LL NEVER LET GO!
LOVEEEEEE
BOOM!

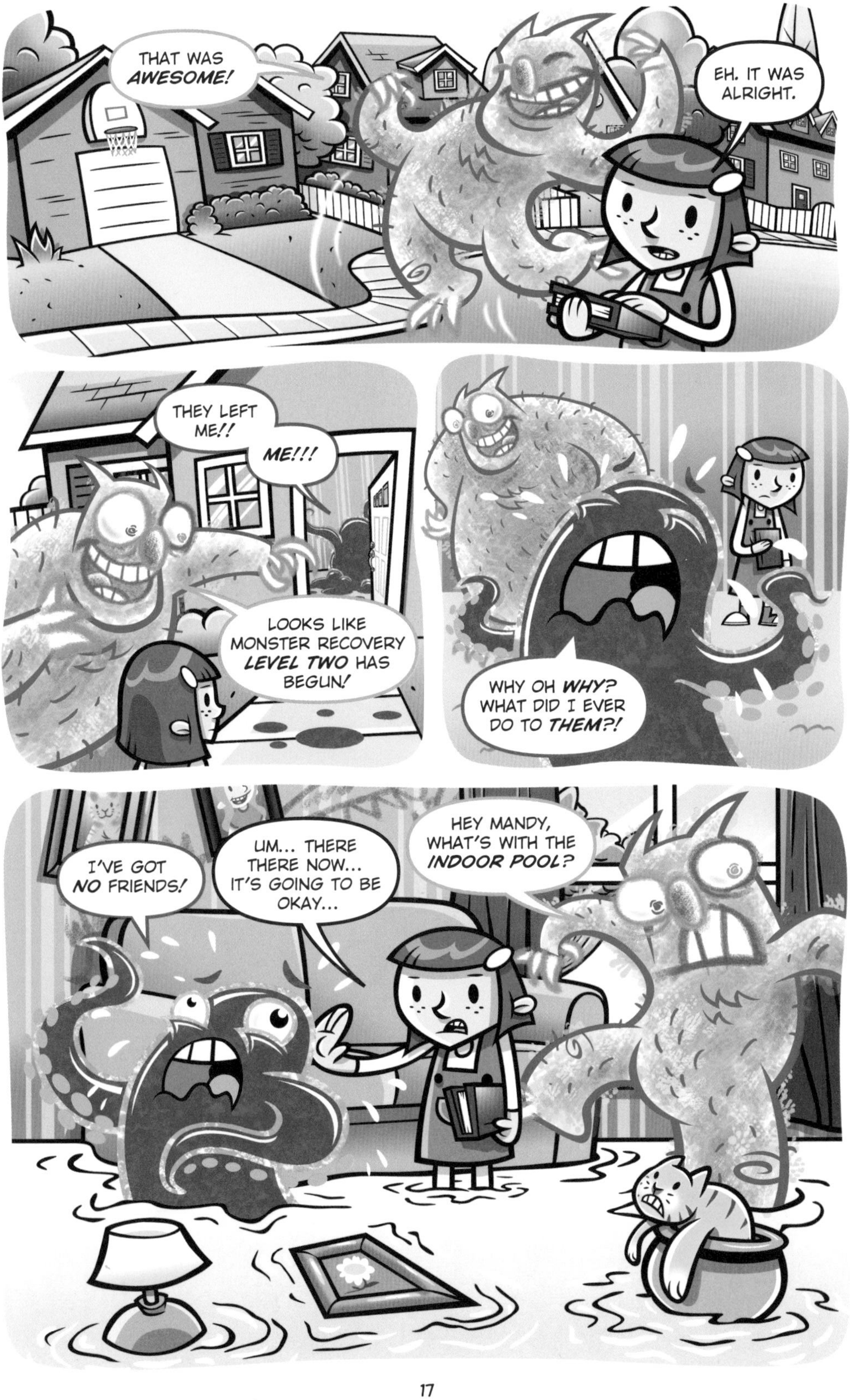
THAT WAS **AWESOME!**
EH. IT WAS ALRIGHT.
THEY LEFT ME!!
ME!!!
LOOKS LIKE MONSTER RECOVERY **LEVEL TWO** HAS BEGUN!
WHY OH **WHY?** WHAT DID I EVER DO TO **THEM?!**
I'VE GOT **NO** FRIENDS!
UM... THERE THERE NOW... IT'S GOING TO BE OKAY...
HEY MANDY, WHAT'S WITH THE **INDOOR POOL?**

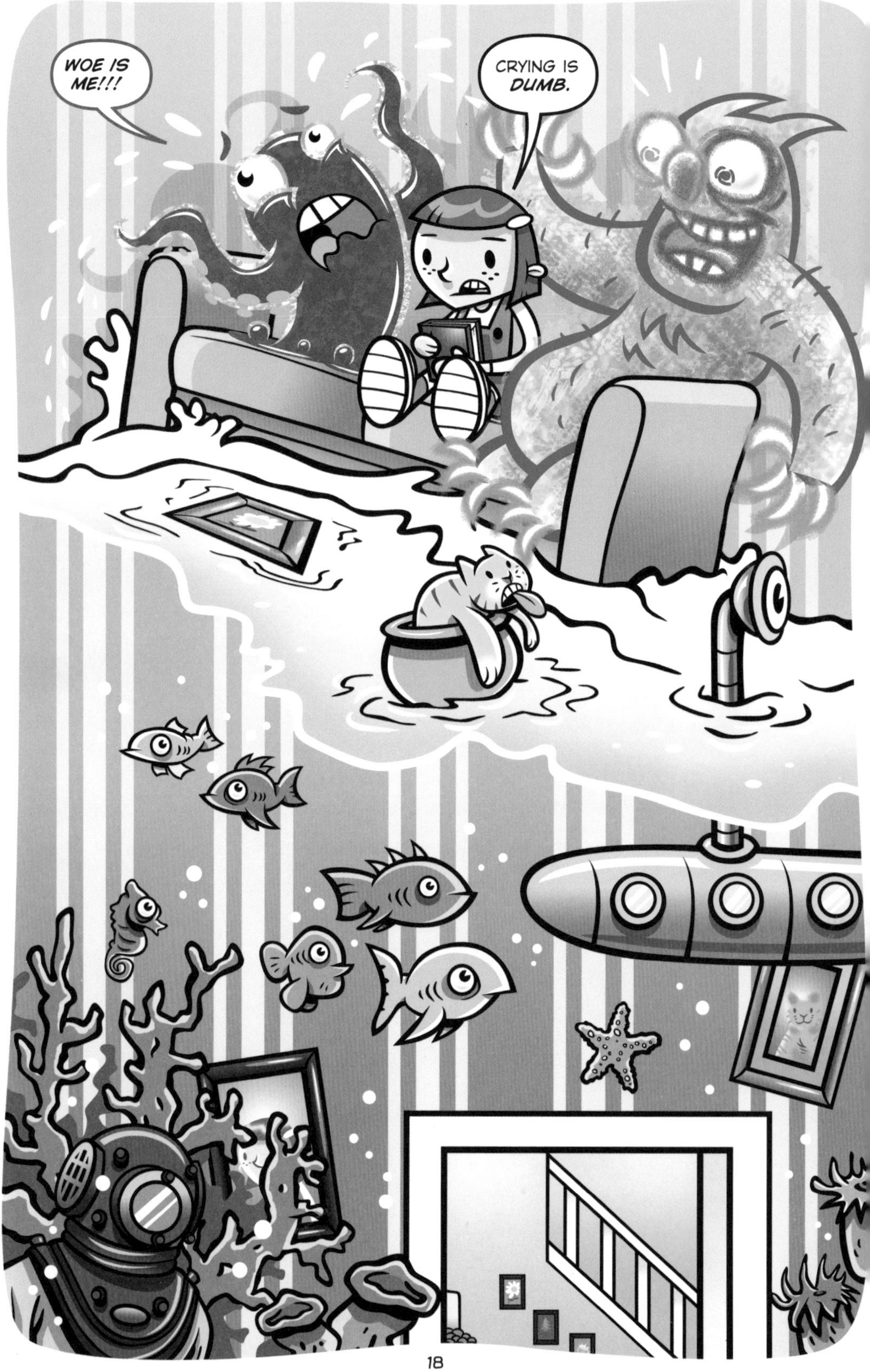
WOE IS ME!!!
CRYING IS DUMB.

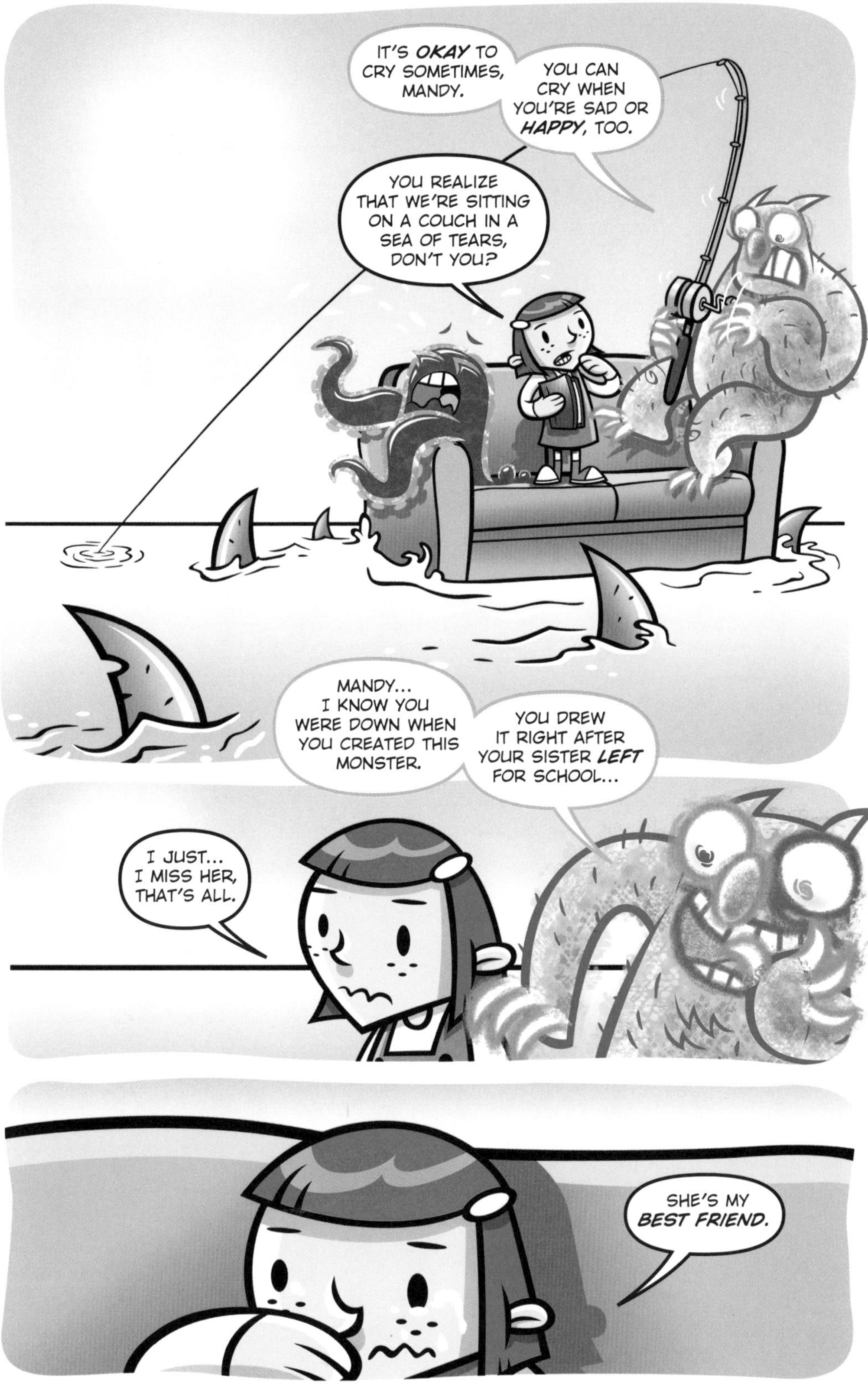
IT'S OKAY TO CRY SOMETIMES, MANDY.
YOU CAN CRY WHEN YOU'RE SAD OR HAPPY, TOO.
YOU REALIZE THAT WE'RE SITTING ON A COUCH IN A SEA OF TEARS, DON'T YOU?
MANDY... I KNOW YOU WERE DOWN WHEN YOU CREATED THIS MONSTER.
YOU DREW IT RIGHT AFTER YOUR SISTER LEFT FOR SCHOOL...
I JUST... I MISS HER, THAT'S ALL.
SHE'S MY BEST FRIEND.

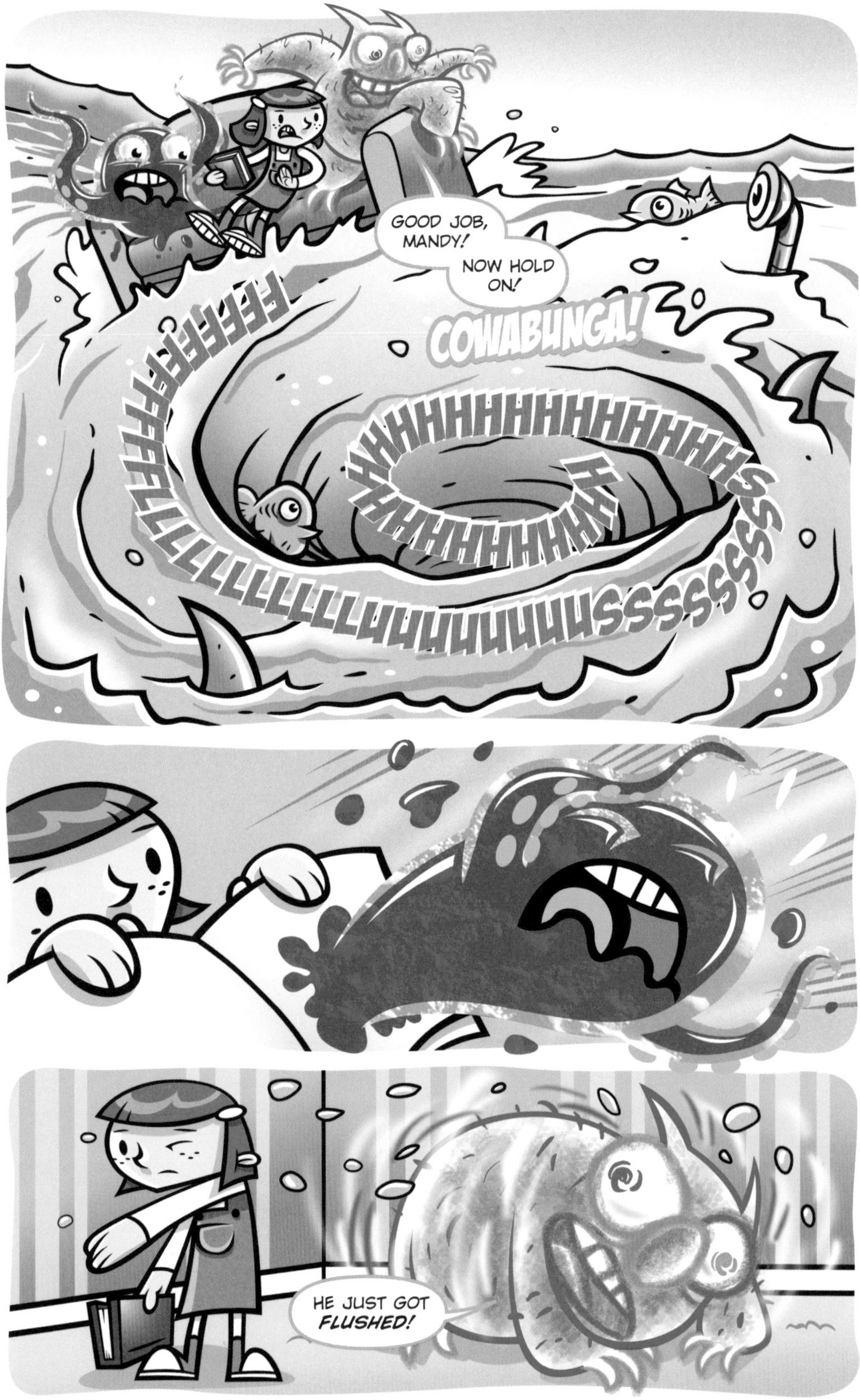
GOOD JOB, MANDY!
NOW HOLD ON!
COWABUNGA!
FFFFFFFFFFLLLLLLLLLLUUUUUUUUUUSSSSSSSSSSHHHHHHHHHHHHHHHHHHHHHHHHHHHHH
HE JUST GOT *FLUSHED!*

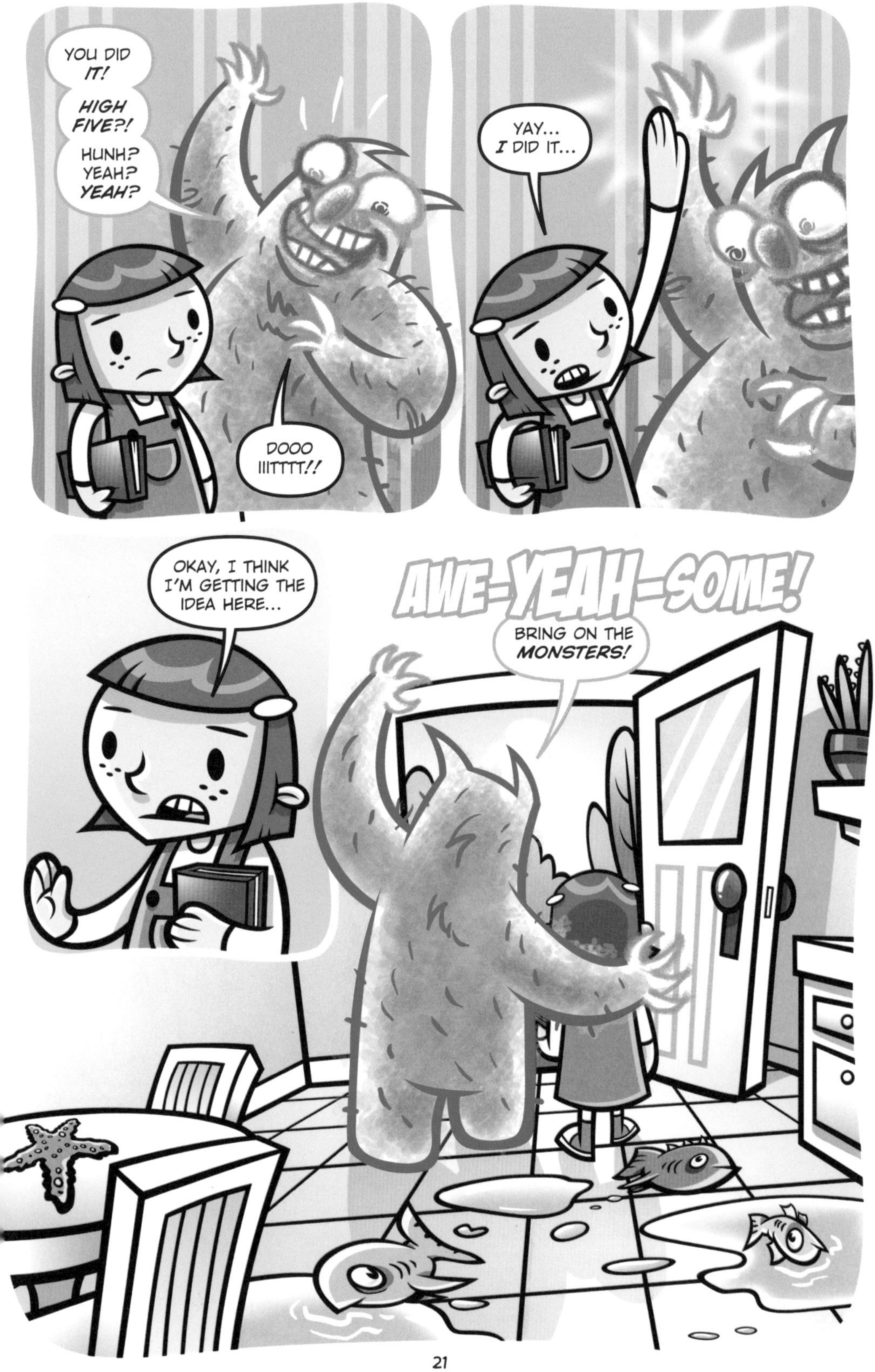
YOU DID IT!
HIGH FIVE?!
HUNH? YEAH? YEAH?
DOOO IIITTTT!!
YAY... I DID IT...
OKAY, I THINK I'M GETTING THE IDEA HERE...
AWE-YEAH-SOME!
BRING ON THE MONSTERS!

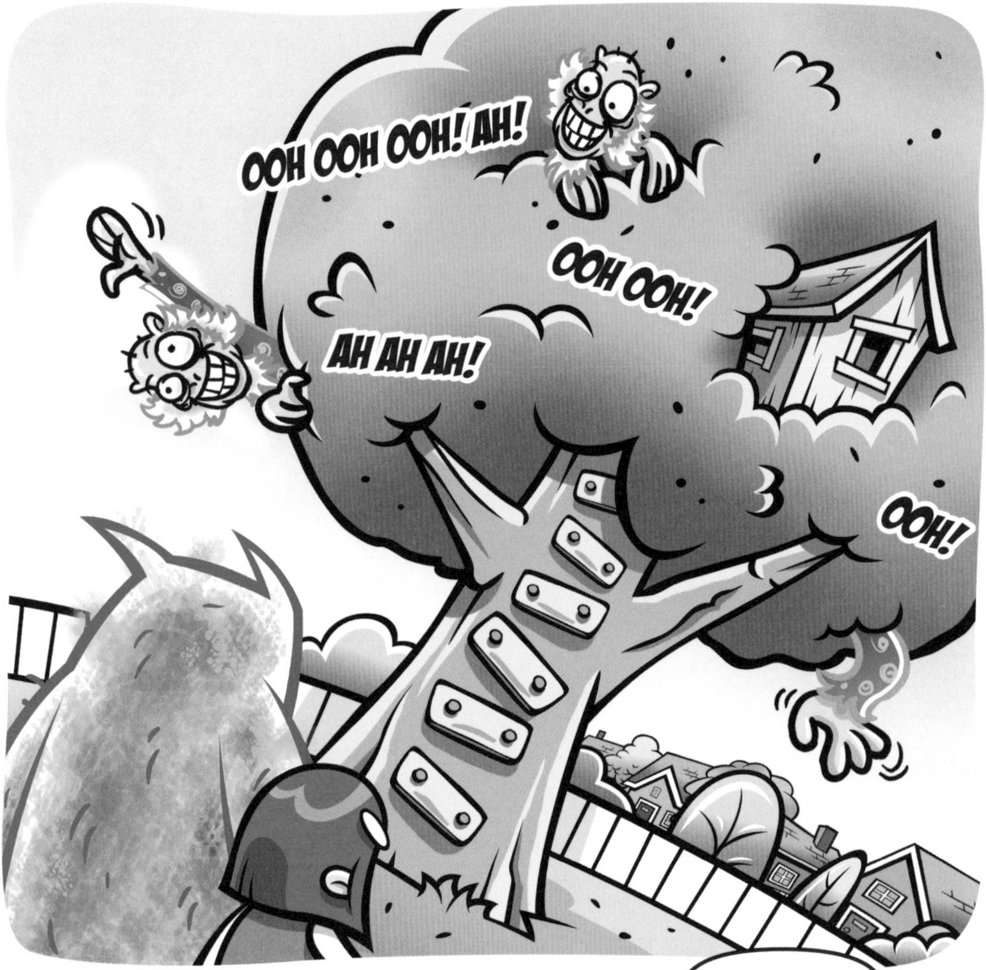
OOH OOH OOH! AH!
OOH OOH!
AH AH AH!
OOH!

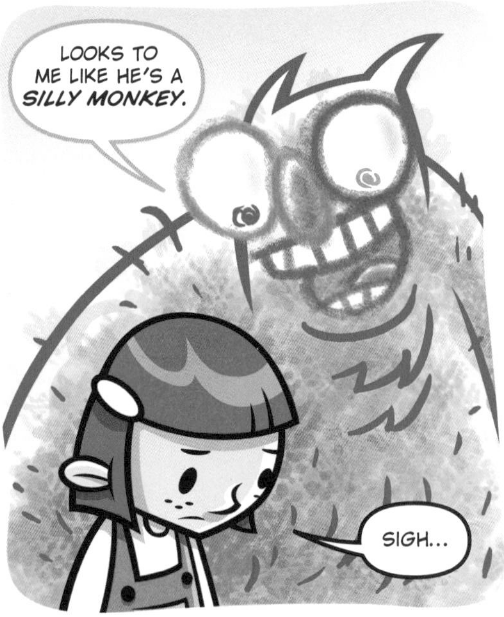
LOOKS TO ME LIKE HE'S A *SILLY MONKEY.*
SIGH...

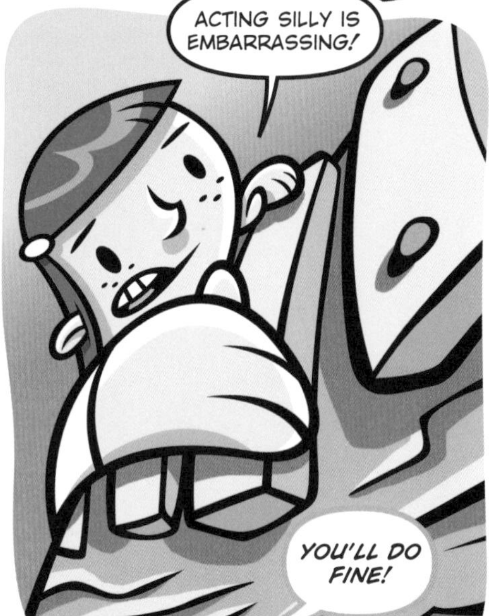
ACTING SILLY IS EMBARRASSING!
YOU'LL DO FINE!

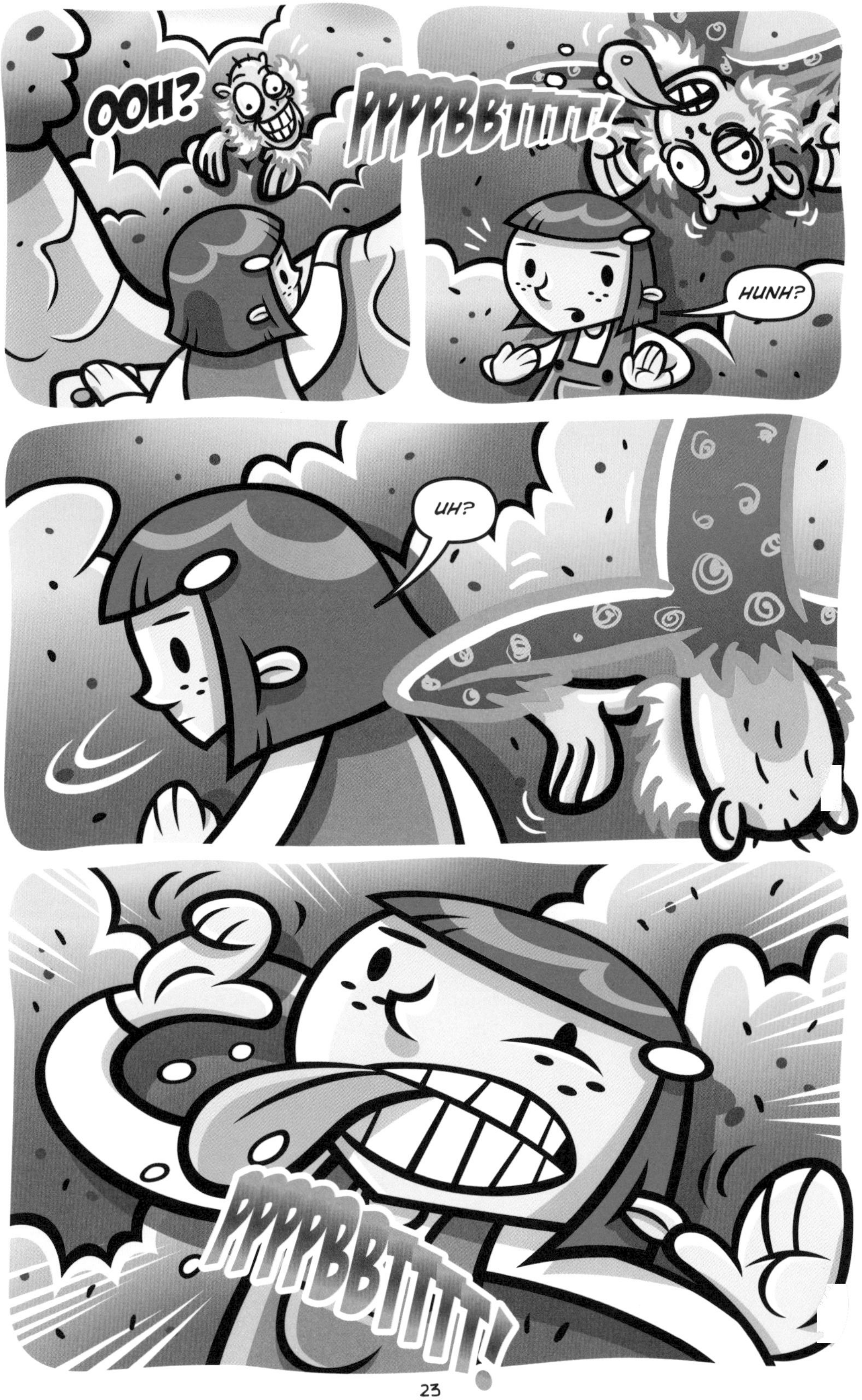
OOH?
PPPPBBTTTTT!
HUNH?
UH?
PPPPBBTTTTT!

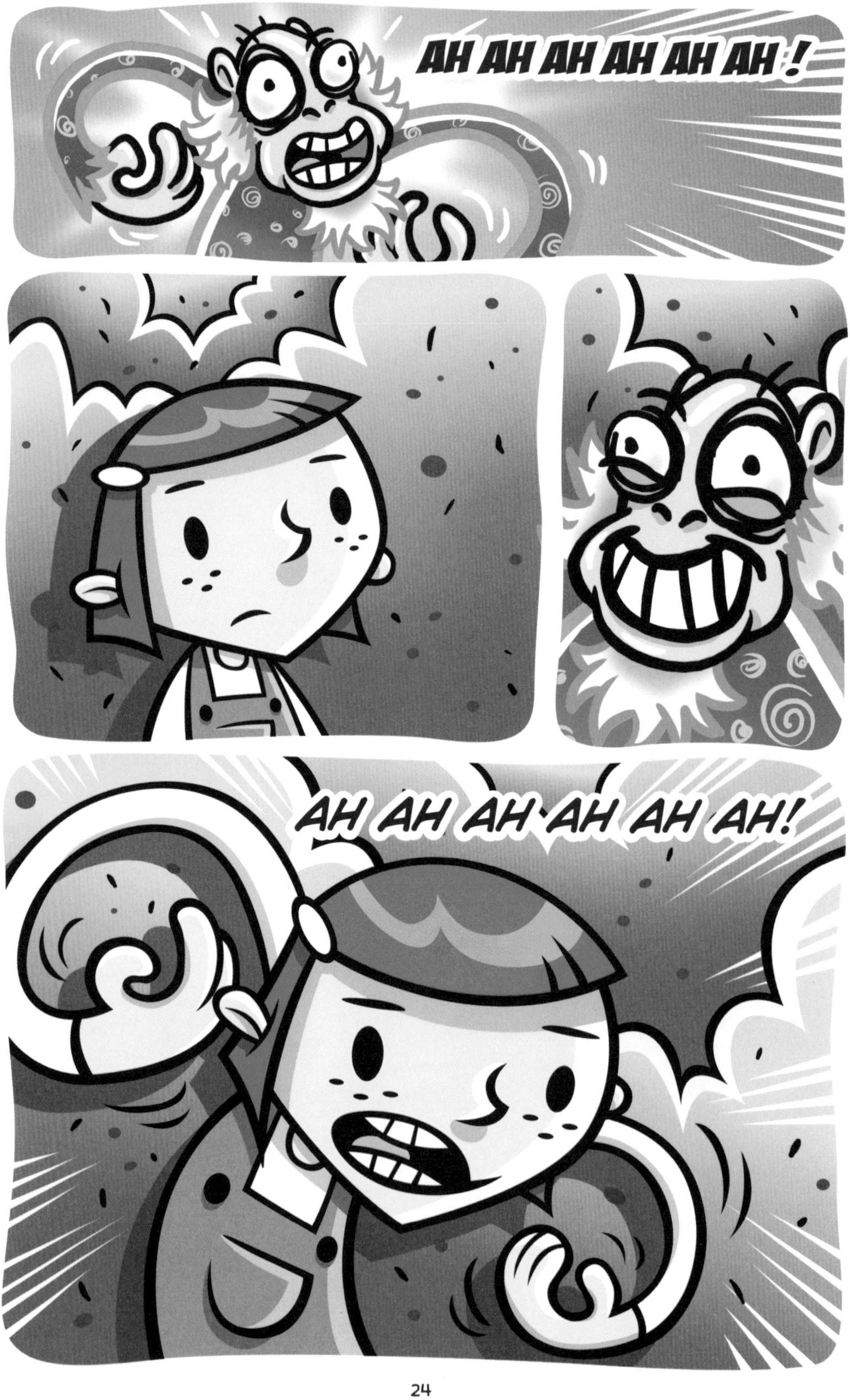
AH AH AH AH AH AH !
AH AH AH AH AH AH!

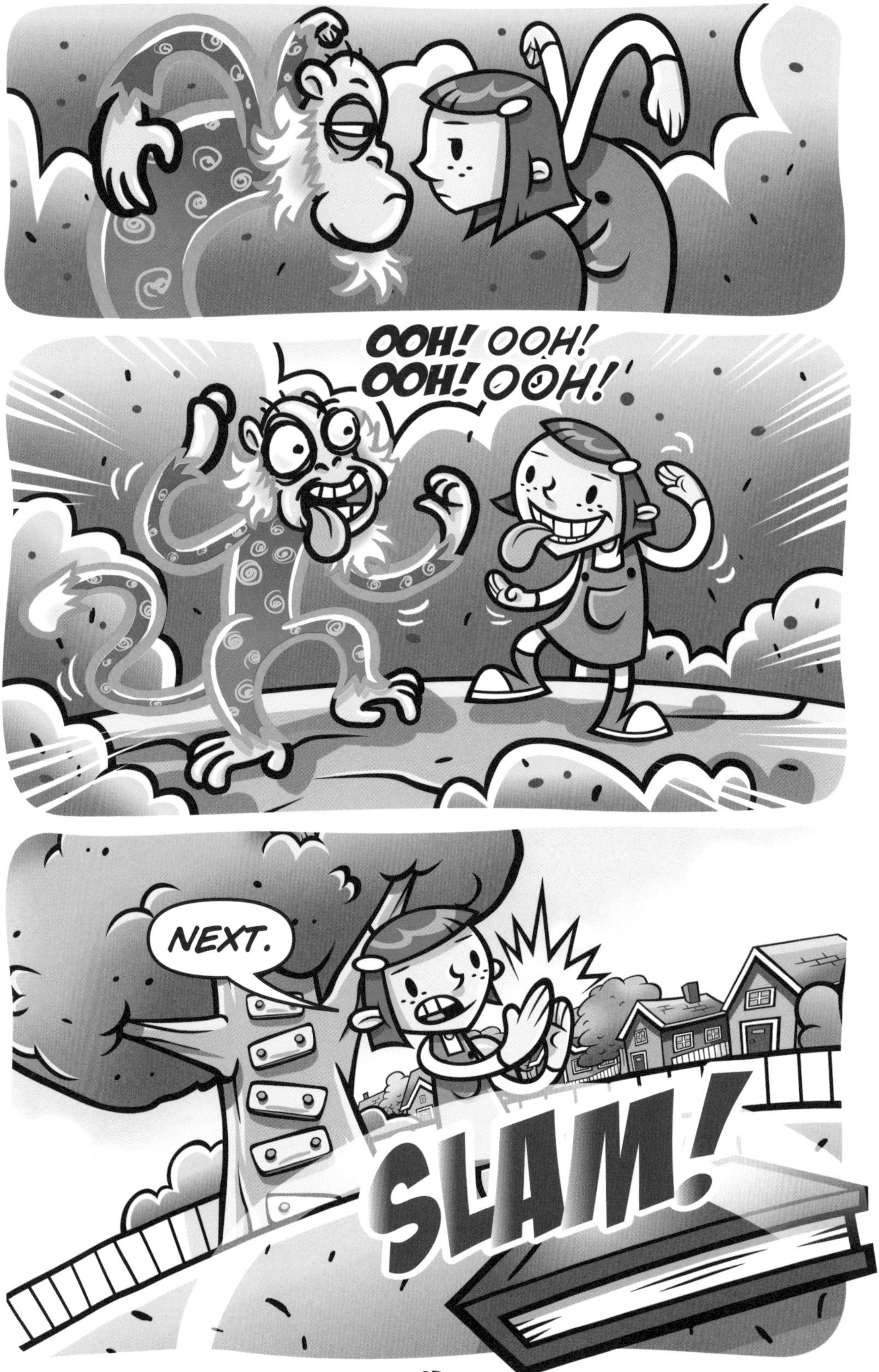
OOH! OOH!
OOH! OOH!
NEXT.
SLAM!

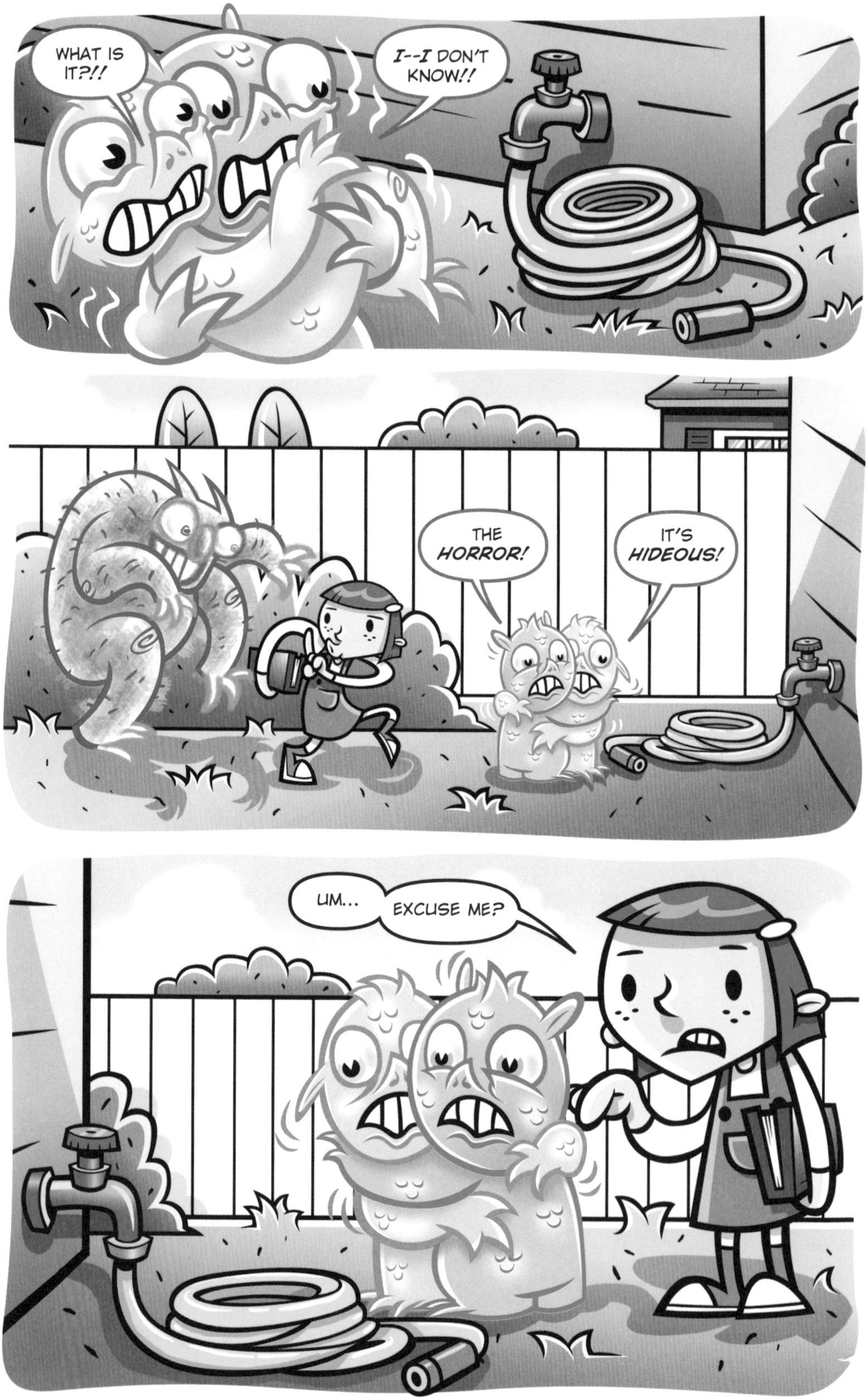
WHAT IS IT?!!
I--I DON'T KNOW!!
THE HORROR!
IT'S HIDEOUS!
UM...
EXCUSE ME?

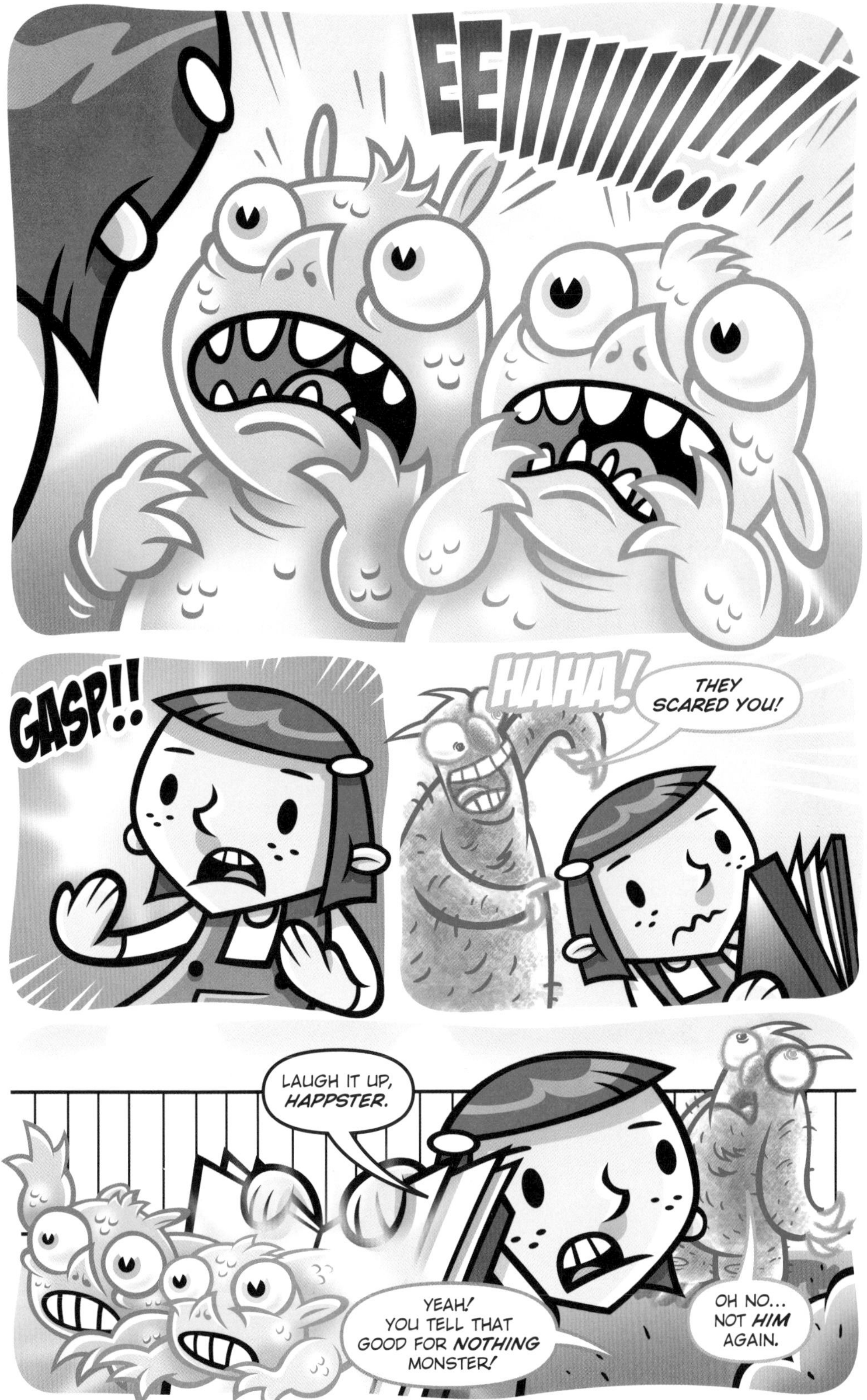
EEIIIIIIIIIII....
GASP!!
HAHA!
THEY SCARED YOU!
LAUGH IT UP, HAPPSTER.
YEAH! YOU TELL THAT GOOD FOR NOTHING MONSTER!
OH NO... NOT HIM AGAIN.

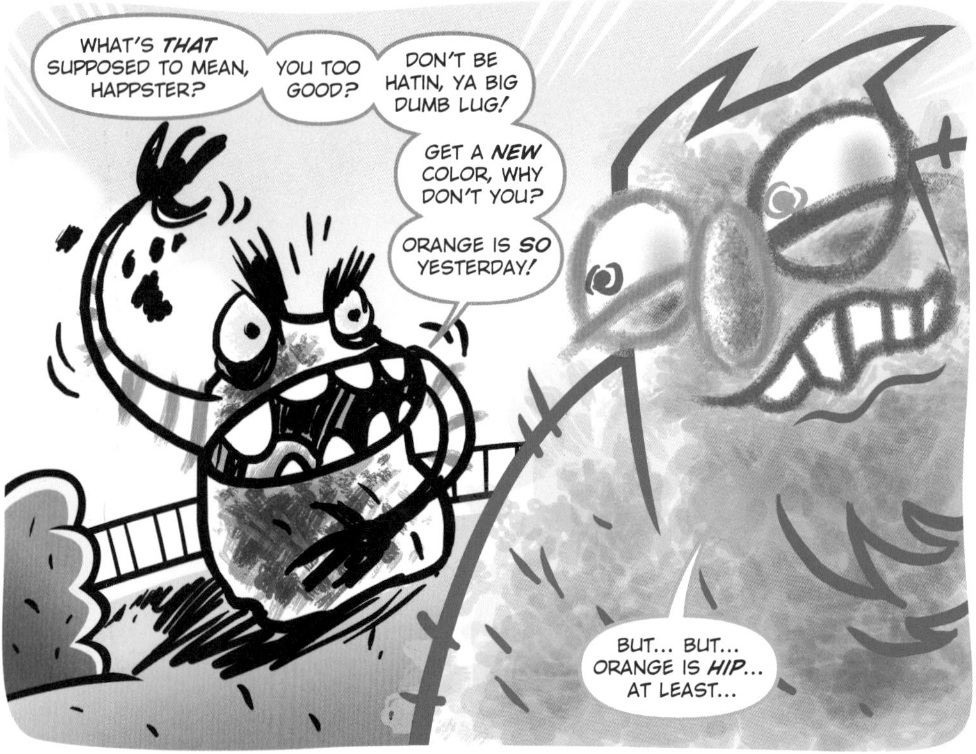
WHAT'S *THAT* SUPPOSED TO MEAN, HAPPSTER?
YOU TOO GOOD?
DON'T BE HATIN, YA BIG DUMB LUG!
GET A *NEW* COLOR, WHY DON'T YOU?
ORANGE IS *SO* YESTERDAY!
BUT... BUT... ORANGE IS *HIP*... AT LEAST...

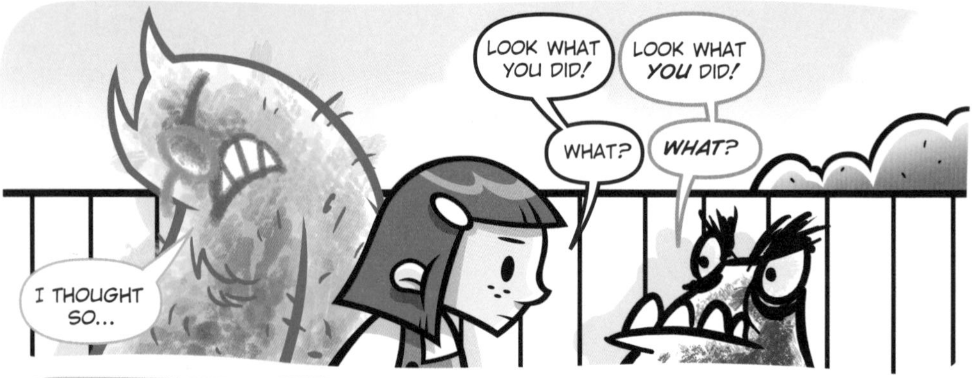
I THOUGHT SO...
LOOK WHAT YOU DID!
LOOK WHAT *YOU* DID!
WHAT?
WHAT?

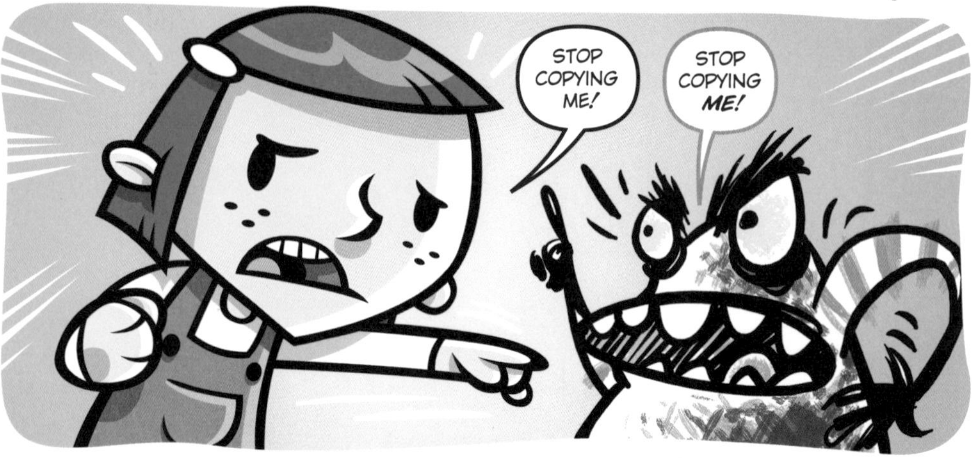
STOP COPYING ME!
STOP COPYING *ME!*

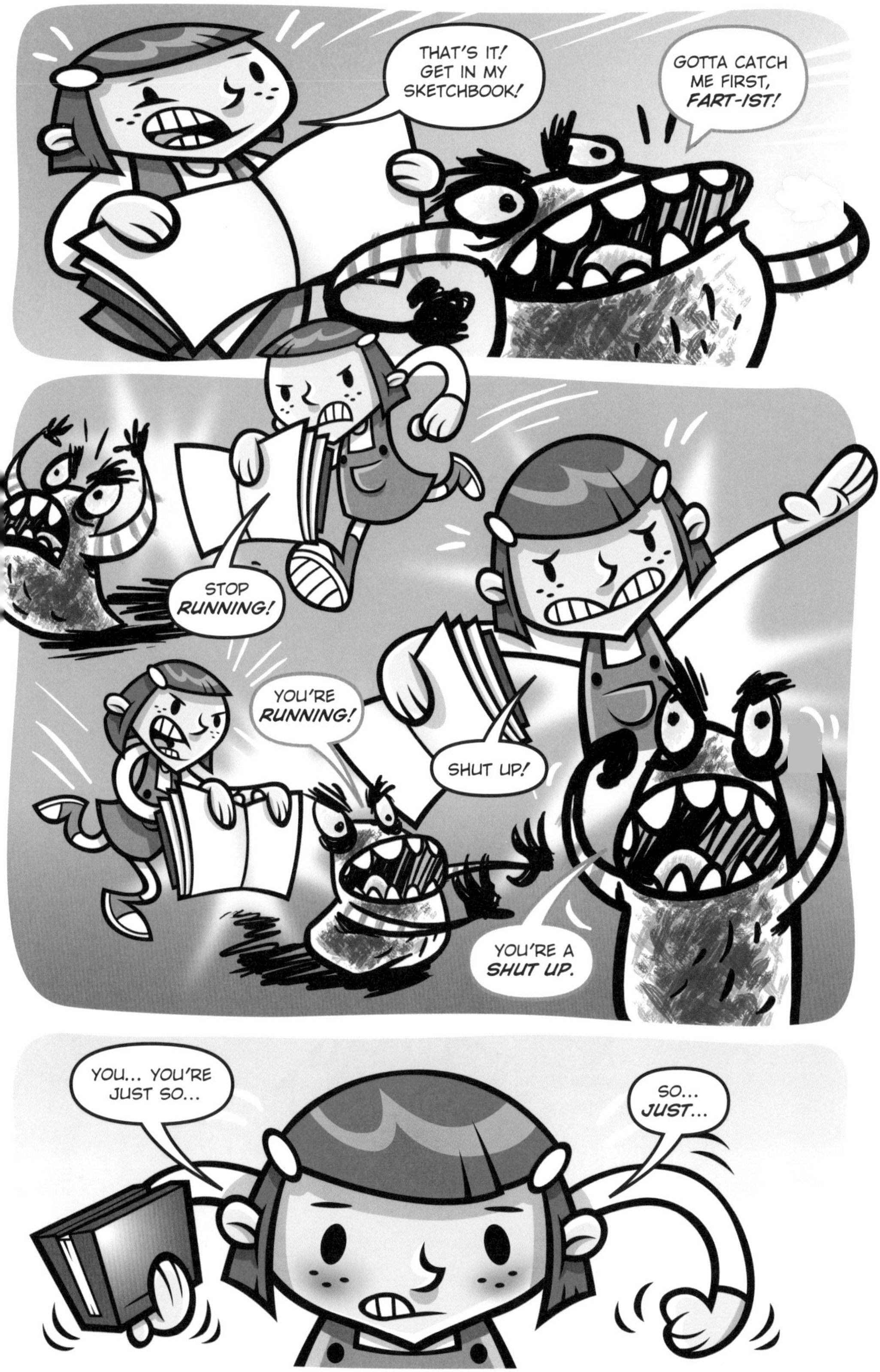
THAT'S IT! GET IN MY SKETCHBOOK!
GOTTA CATCH ME FIRST, FART-IST!
STOP RUNNING!
YOU'RE RUNNING!
SHUT UP!
YOU'RE A SHUT UP.
YOU... YOU'RE JUST SO...
SO... JUST...

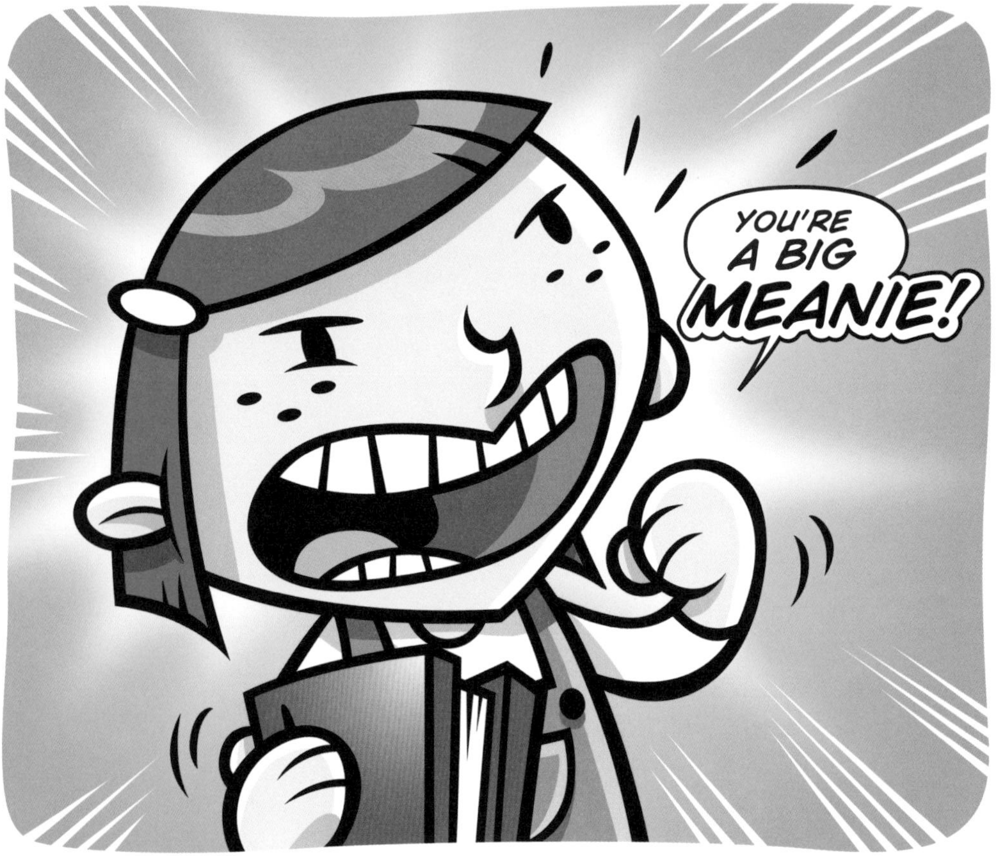
YOU'RE A BIG MEANIE!

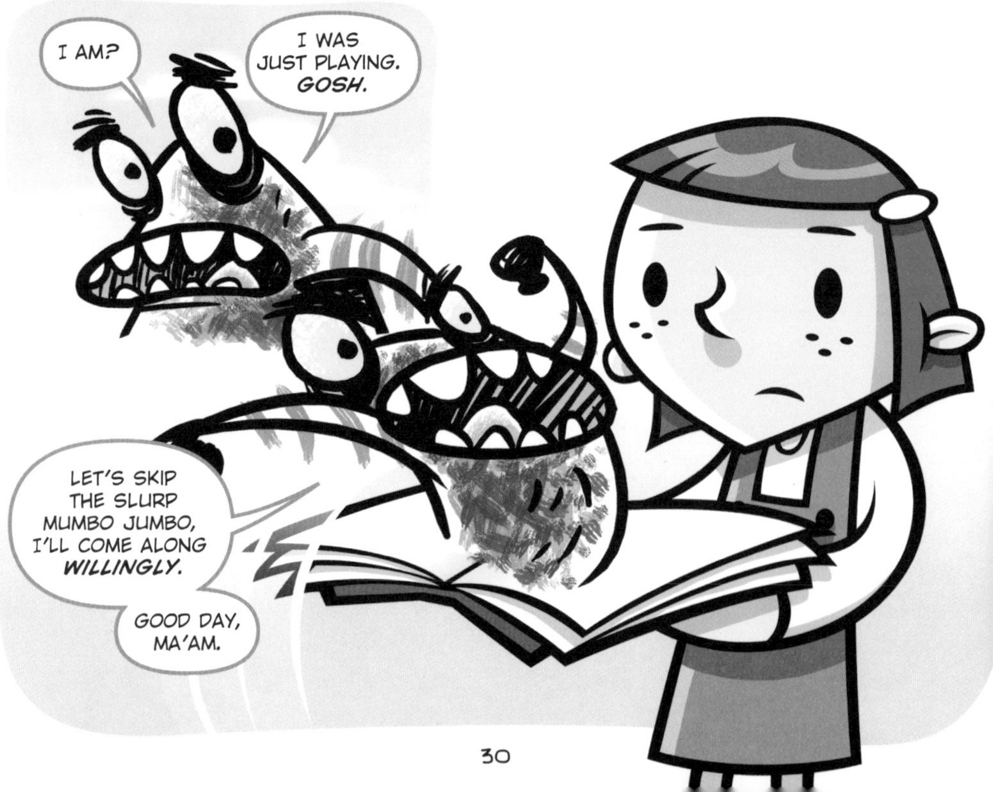
I AM?
I WAS JUST PLAYING. GOSH.
LET'S SKIP THE SLURP MUMBO JUMBO, I'LL COME ALONG WILLINGLY.
GOOD DAY, MA'AM.

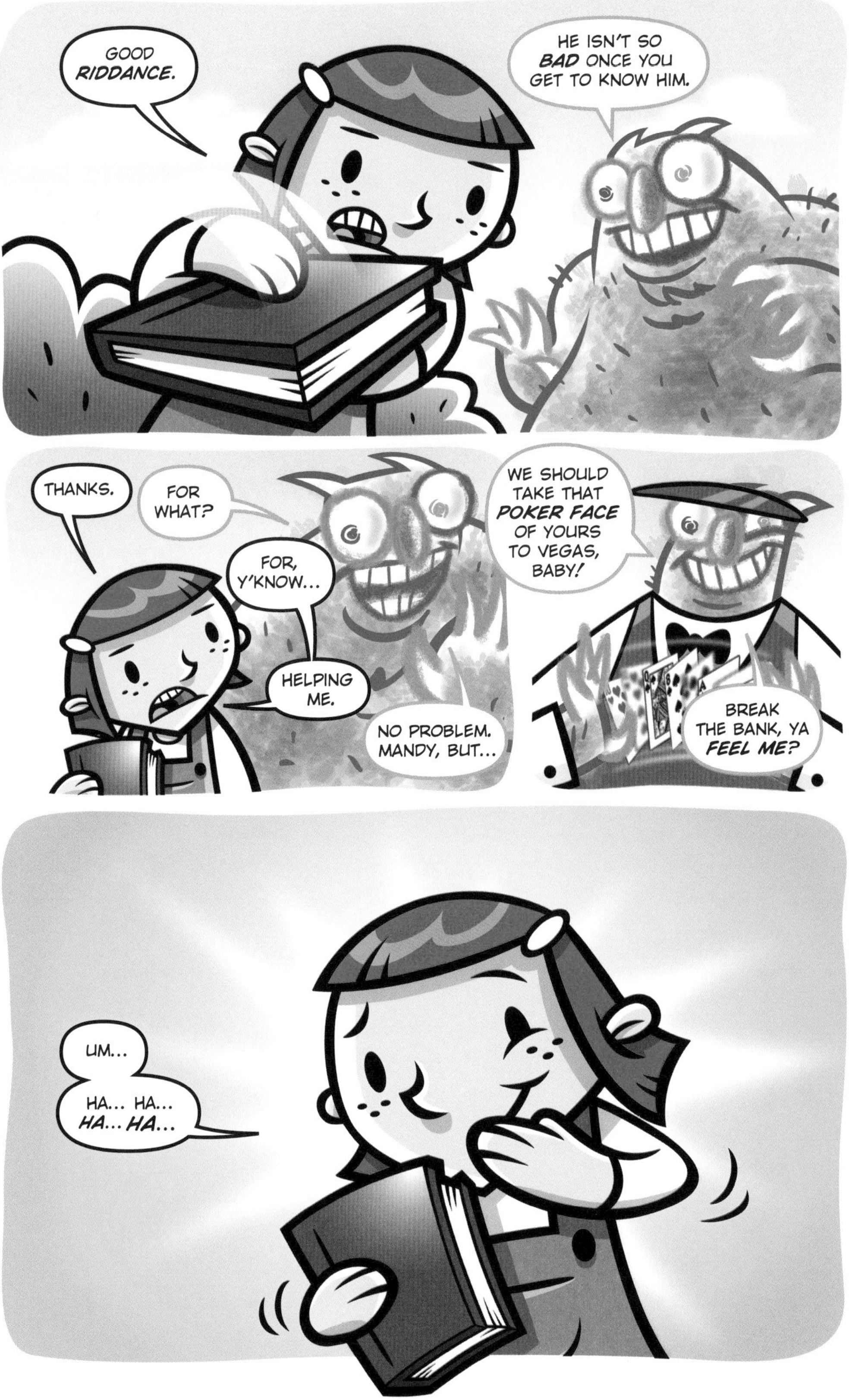

GOOD RIDDANCE.
HE ISN'T SO BAD ONCE YOU GET TO KNOW HIM.
THANKS.
FOR WHAT?
FOR, Y'KNOW...
HELPING ME.
NO PROBLEM. MANDY, BUT...
WE SHOULD TAKE THAT POKER FACE OF YOURS TO VEGAS, BABY!
BREAK THE BANK, YA FEEL ME?
UM...
HA... HA... HA... HA...

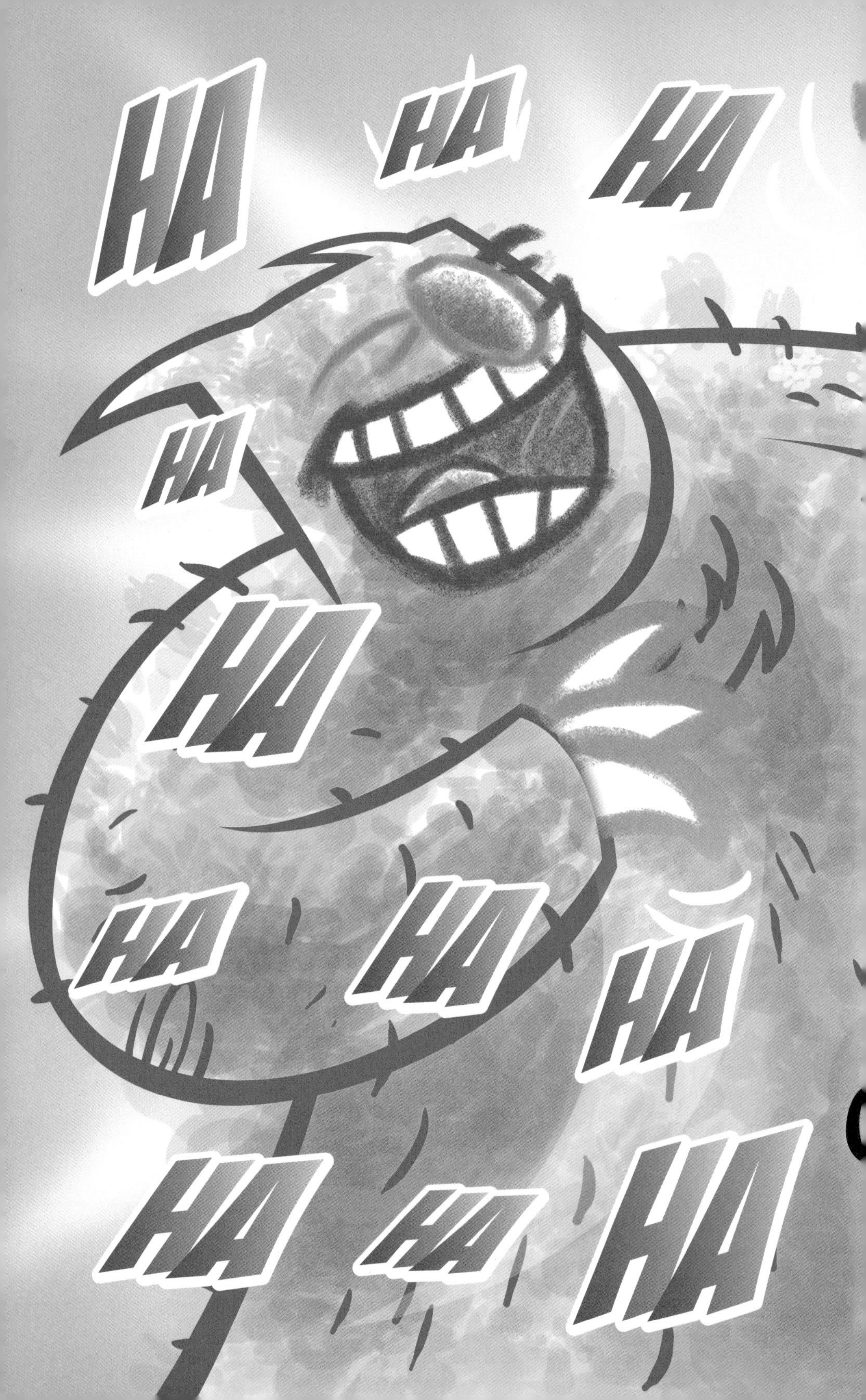
HA
HA
HA
HA
HA
HA
HA
HA
HA
HA
HA

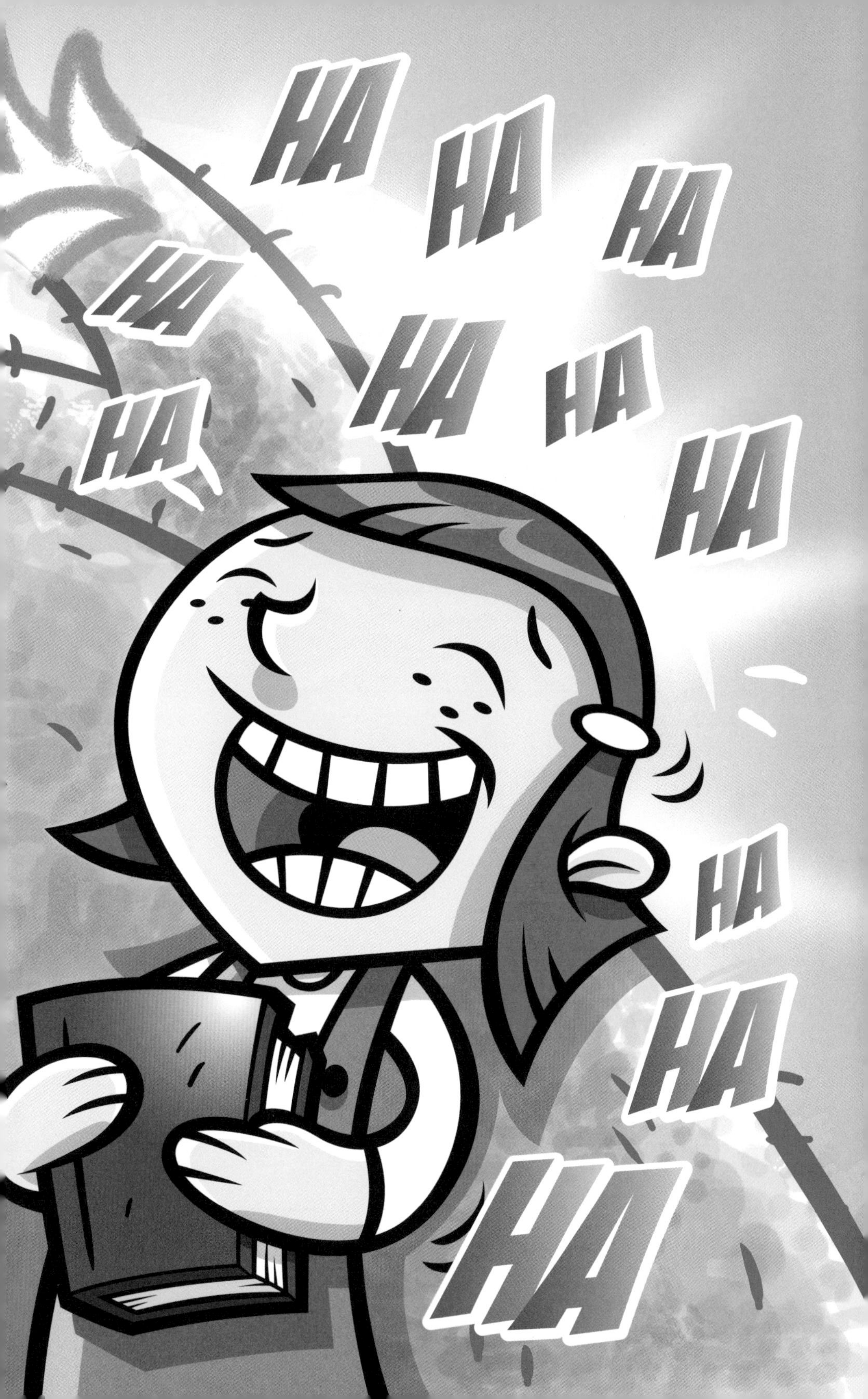
HA
HA
HA
HA
HA
HA
HA
HA
HA
HA
HA

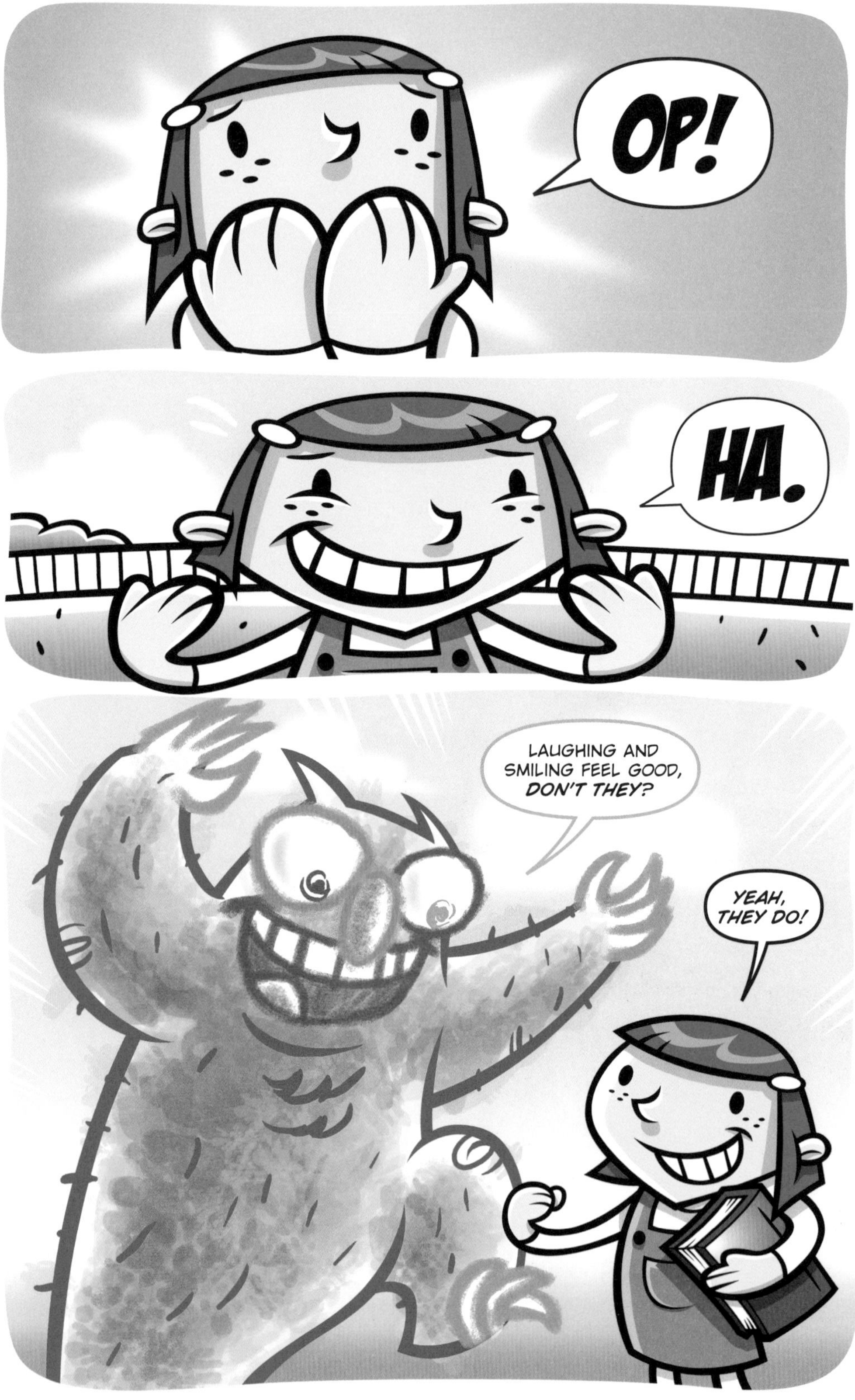
OP!
HA.
LAUGHING AND SMILING FEEL GOOD, *DON'T THEY?*
YEAH, THEY DO!

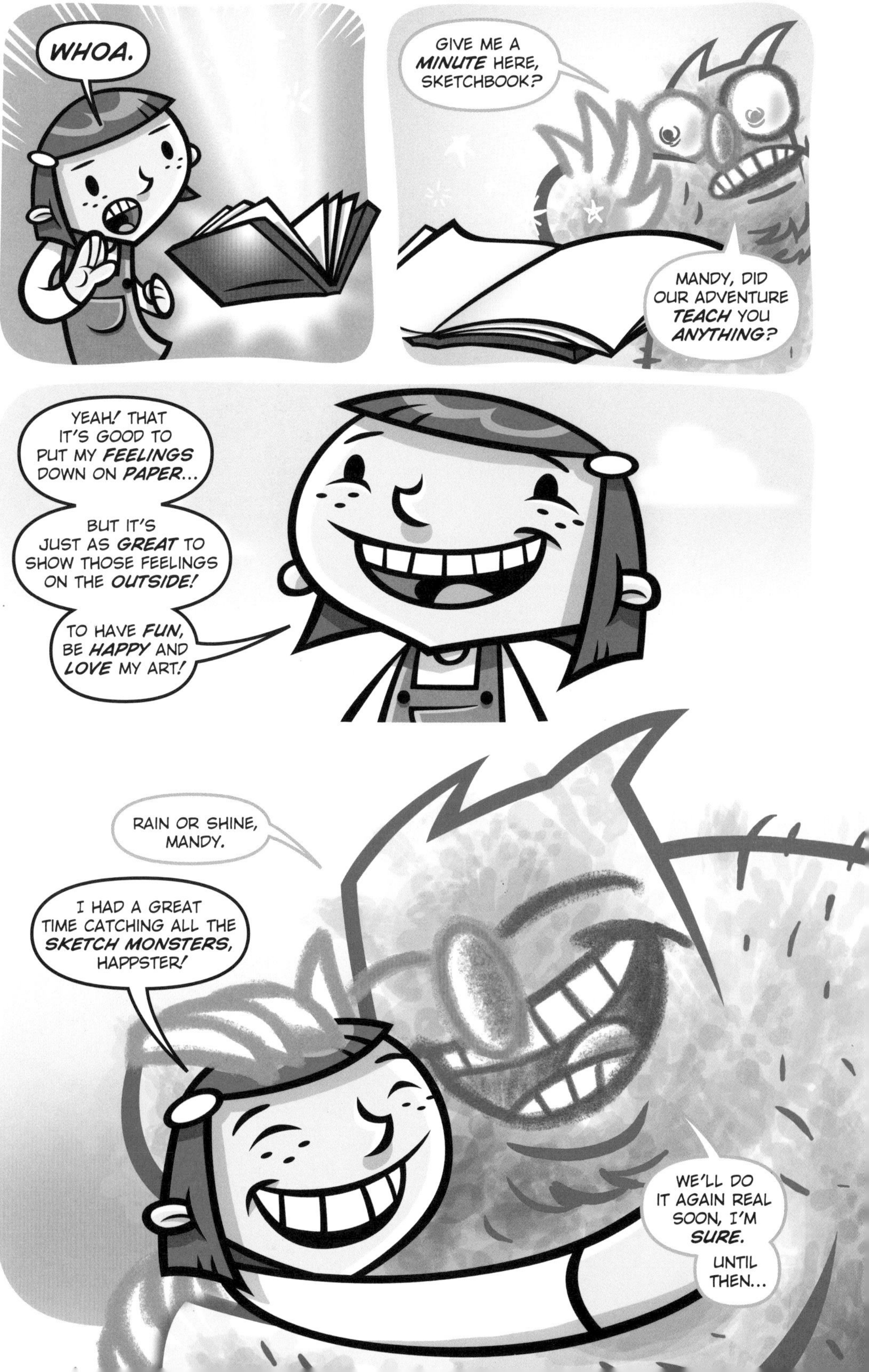
WHOA.
GIVE ME A MINUTE HERE, SKETCHBOOK?
MANDY, DID OUR ADVENTURE TEACH YOU ANYTHING?
YEAH! THAT IT'S GOOD TO PUT MY FEELINGS DOWN ON PAPER...
BUT IT'S JUST AS GREAT TO SHOW THOSE FEELINGS ON THE OUTSIDE!
TO HAVE FUN, BE HAPPY AND LOVE MY ART!
RAIN OR SHINE, MANDY.
I HAD A GREAT TIME CATCHING ALL THE SKETCH MONSTERS, HAPPSTER!
WE'LL DO IT AGAIN REAL SOON, I'M SURE.
UNTIL THEN...

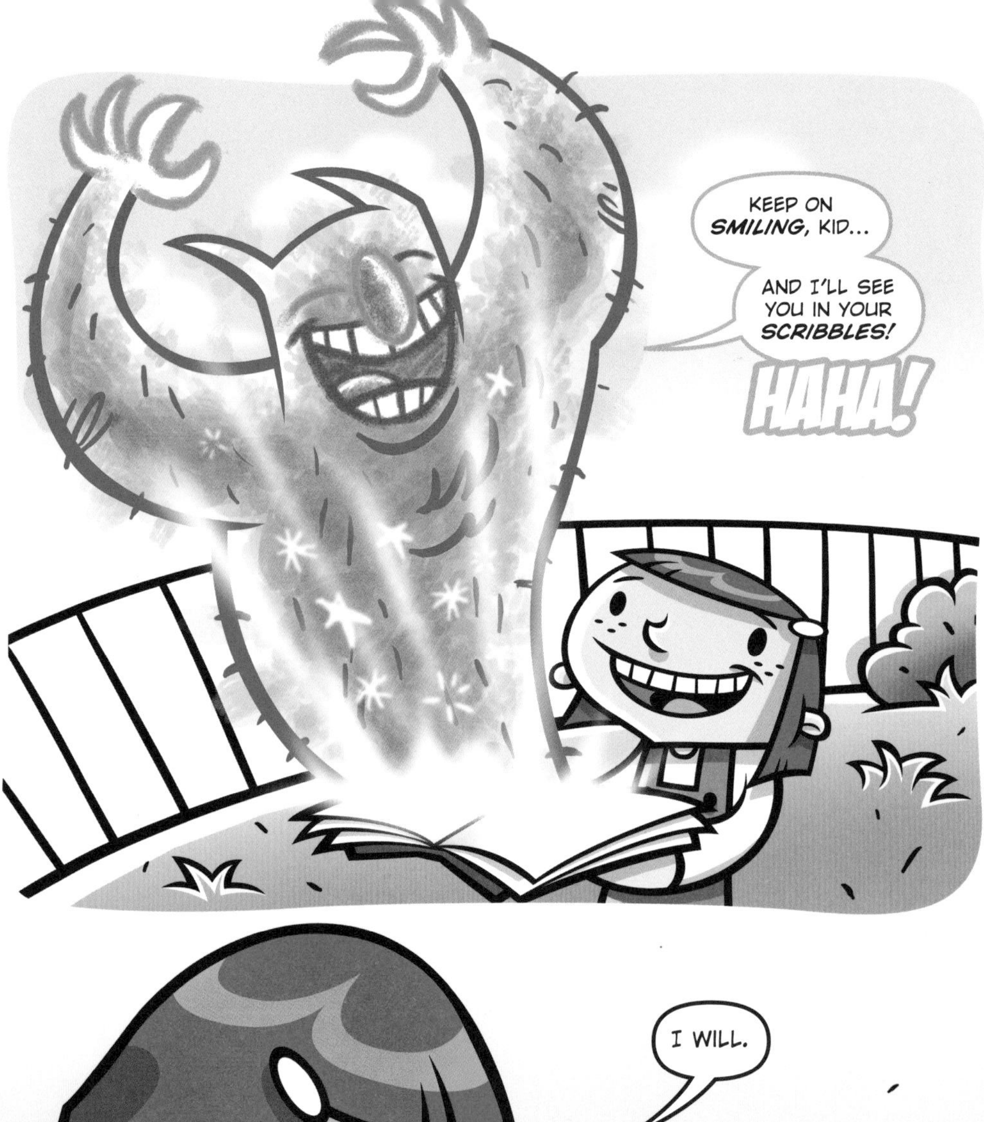
KEEP ON SMILING, KID...
AND I'LL SEE YOU IN YOUR SCRIBBLES!
HAHA!

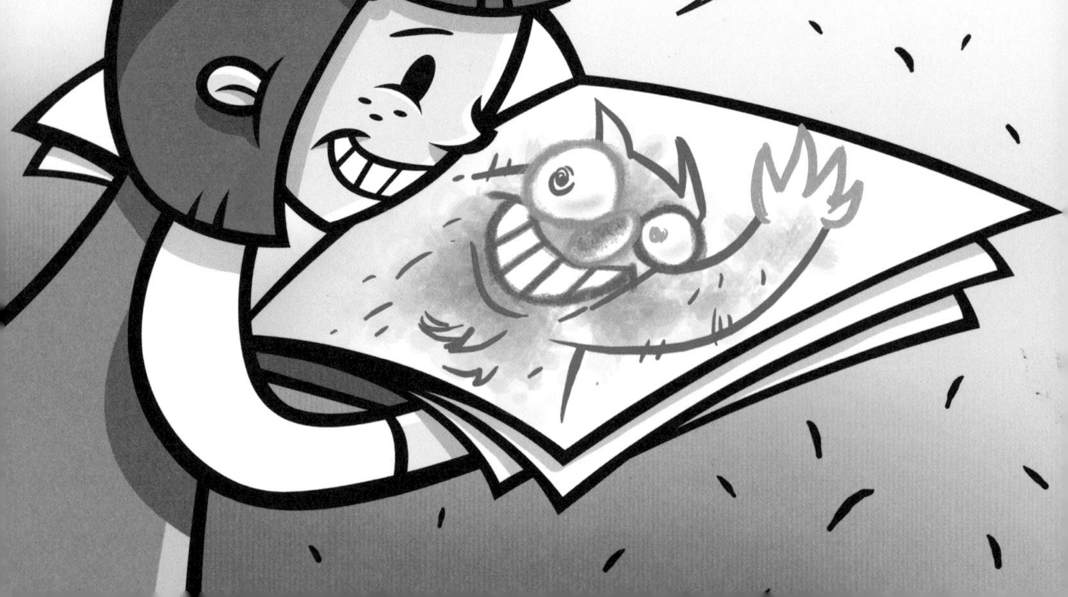
I WILL.

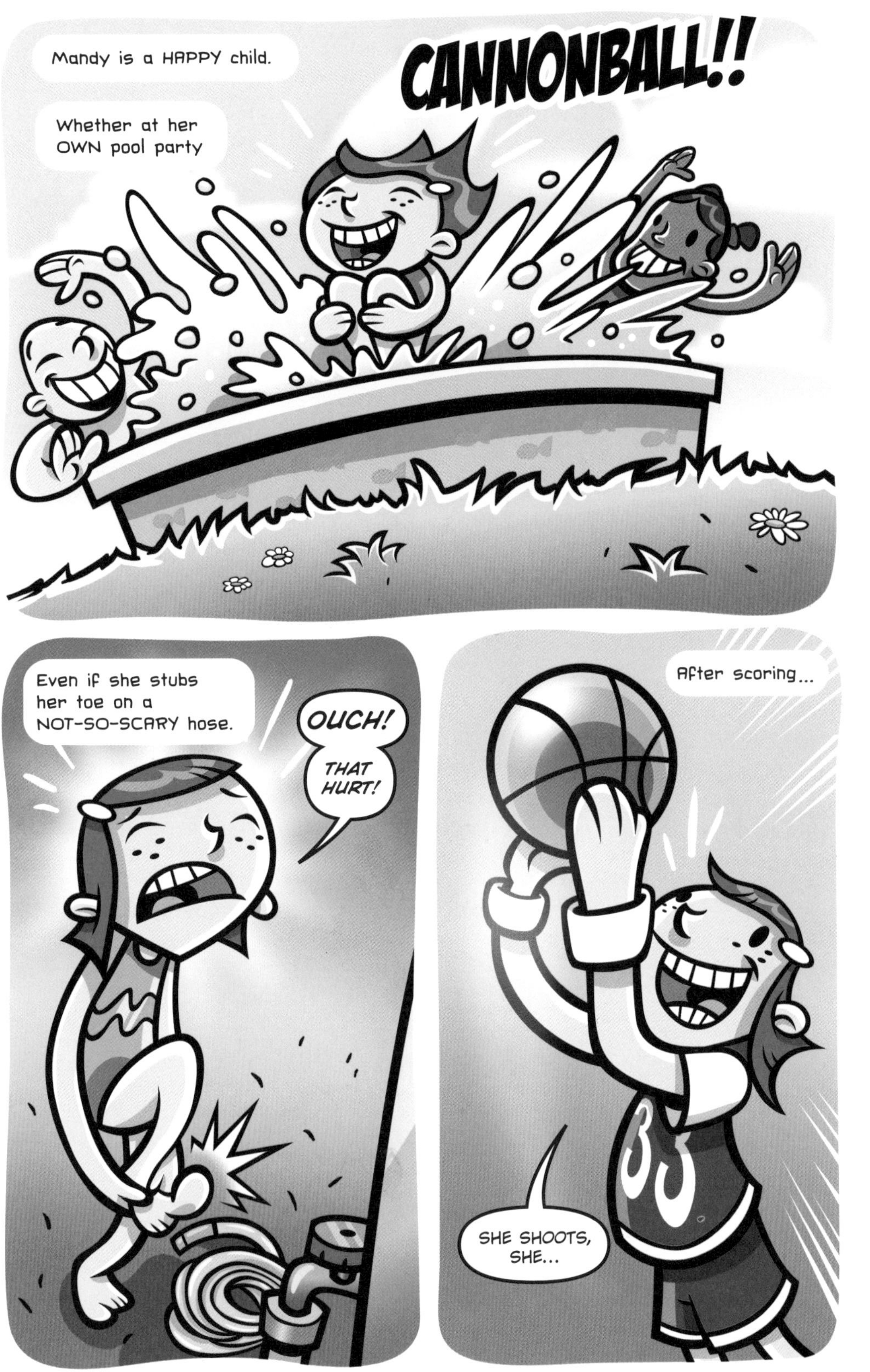
Mandy is a HAPPY child.
CANNONBALL!!
Whether at her OWN pool party
Even if she stubs her toe on a NOT-SO-SCARY hose.
OUCH!
THAT HURT!
After scoring...
SHE SHOOTS, SHE...

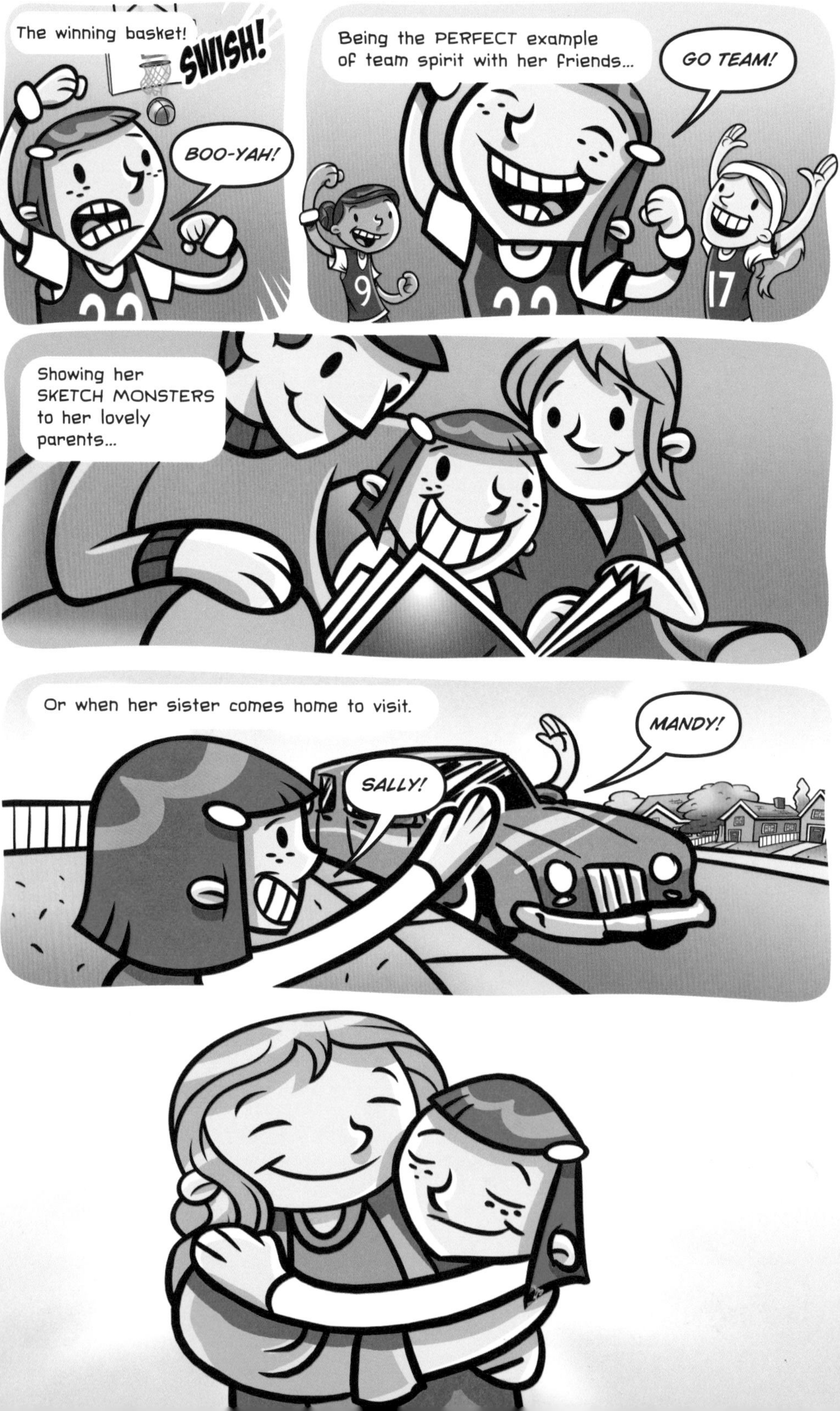
The winning basket!
SWISH!
BOO-YAH!
Being the PERFECT example of team spirit with her friends...
GO TEAM!
Showing her SKETCH MONSTERS to her lovely parents...
Or when her sister comes home to visit.
SALLY!
MANDY!

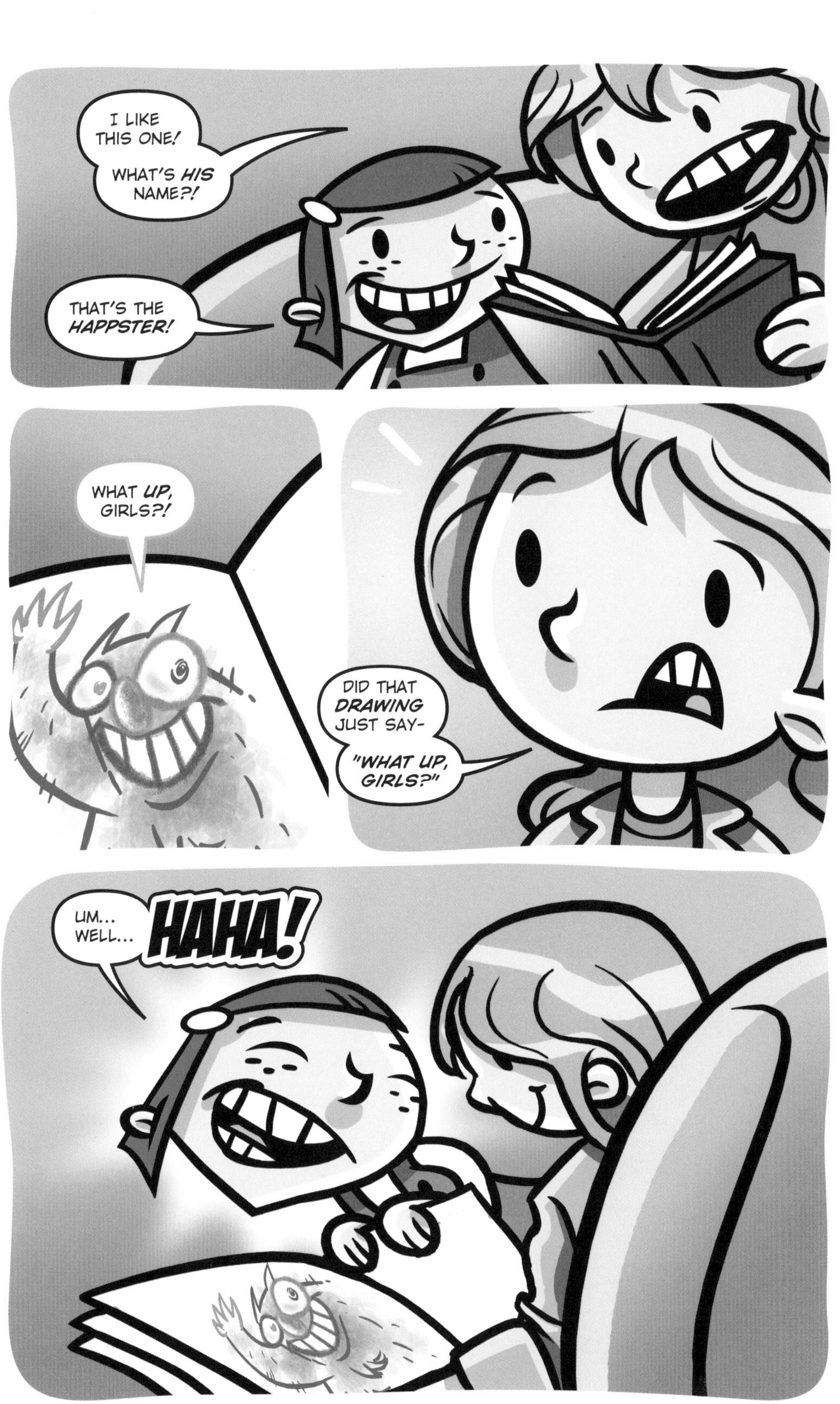
I LIKE THIS ONE!
WHAT'S HIS NAME?!
THAT'S THE HAPPSTER!
WHAT UP, GIRLS?!
DID THAT DRAWING JUST SAY-
"WHAT UP, GIRLS?"
UM... WELL...
HAHA!

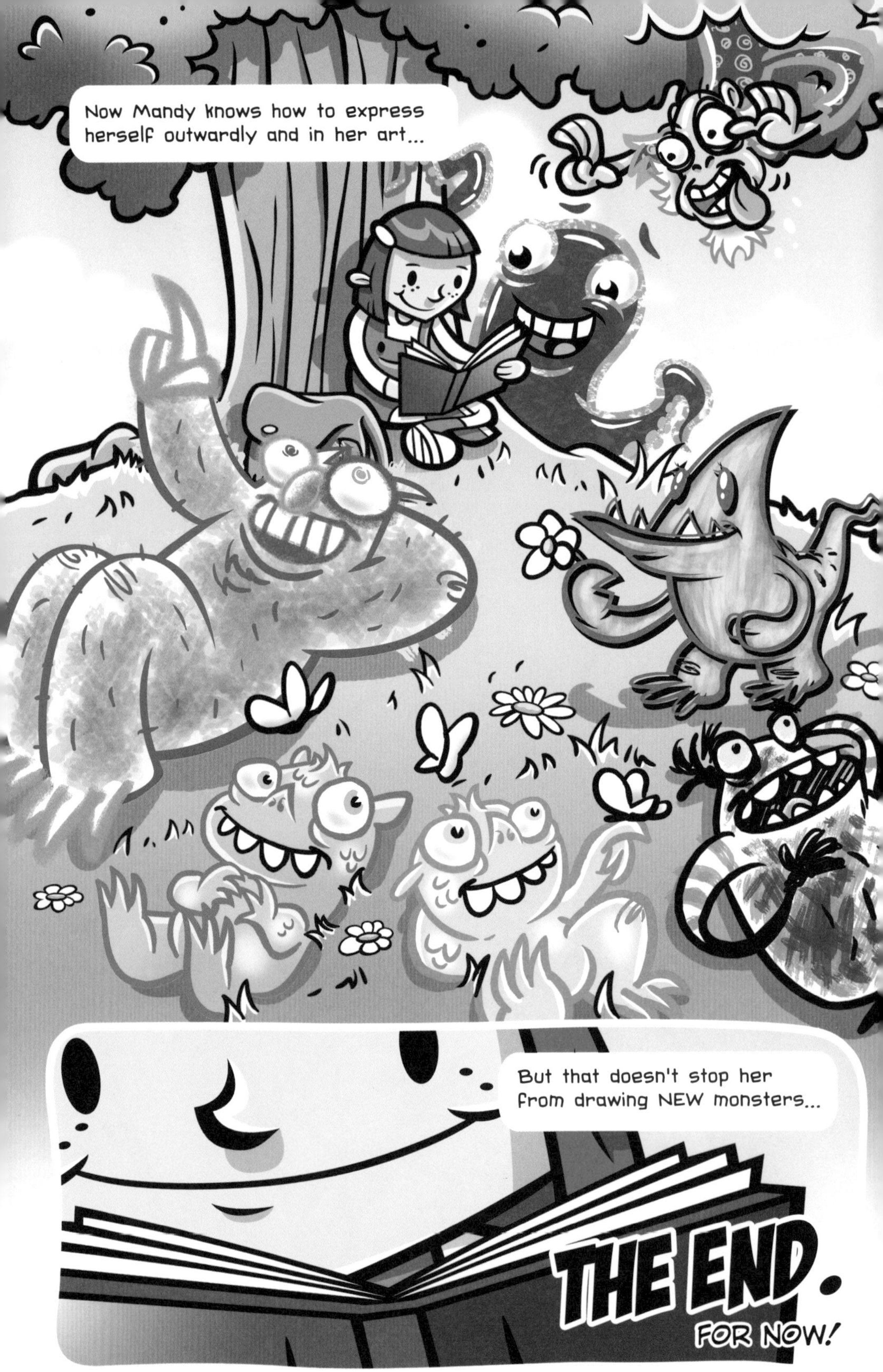
Now Mandy knows how to express herself outwardly and in her art...
But that doesn't stop her from drawing NEW monsters...
THE END.
FOR NOW!

SKETCHIN' SKETCH MONSTERS

When Vinny first starts working on a page of Sketch Monsters, he uses a black pen to draw everything in his sketchbook while he's working out the details. When he is finished drawing in pen he then scans his drawings from his sketchbook and inks and colors over his drawings using the computer.

Here are some examples of his pen drawings inside his sketchbook for Sketch Monsters.

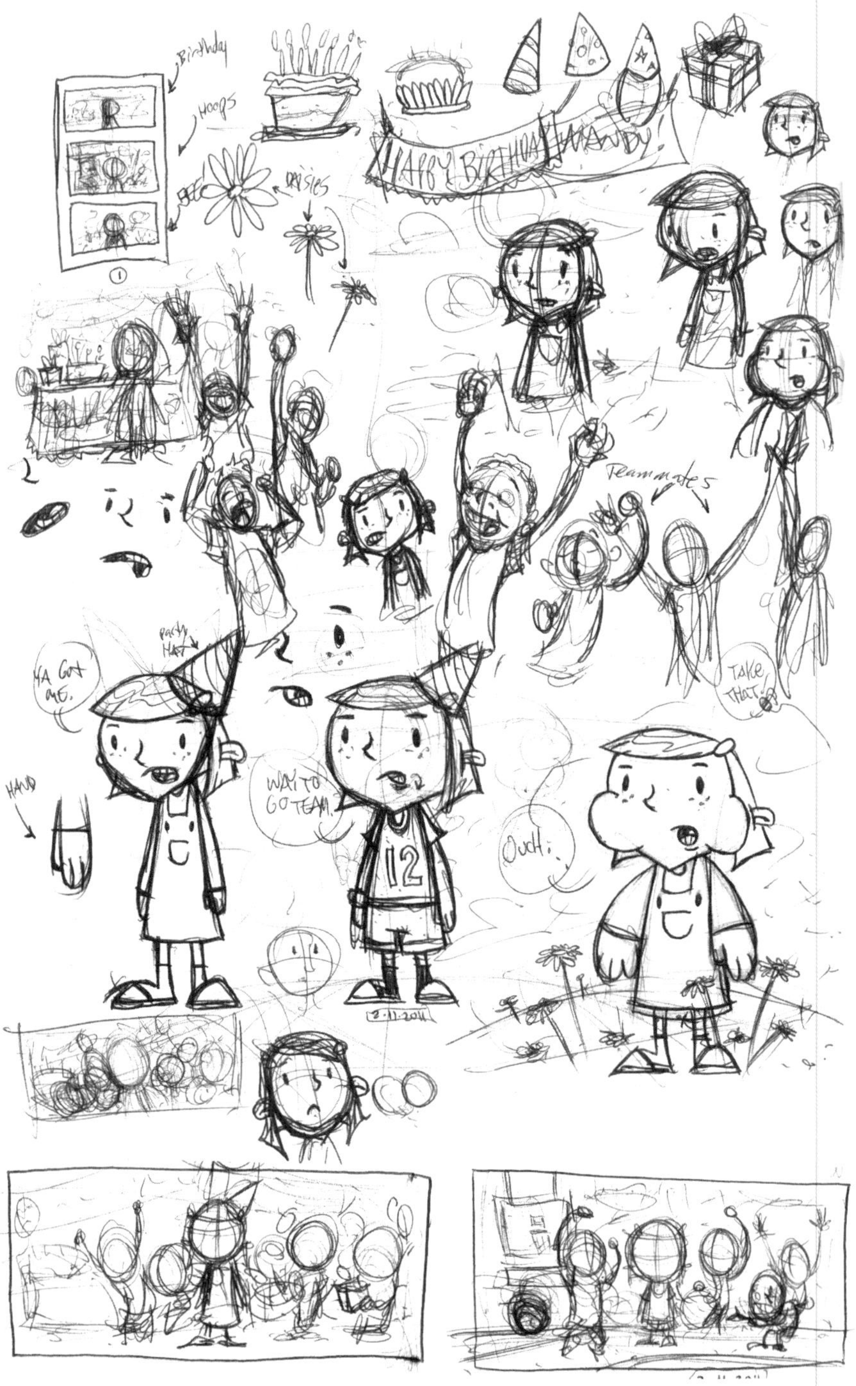
Birthday
Hoops
Daisies
HAPPY BIRTHDAY MANDY!
Teammates
Party Hat
YA GOT ME.
HAND
WAY TO GO TEAM.
12
Ouch!
TAKE THAT!

Here are some of Vinny's sample drawings for characters that would appear in the pages of the book. Below are rough panel layouts for what would become panel one and two of the first page of the book.

These are some of the possible designs for Mandy that Vinny drew in the beginning.
Can you spot which one he decided to use for the book?

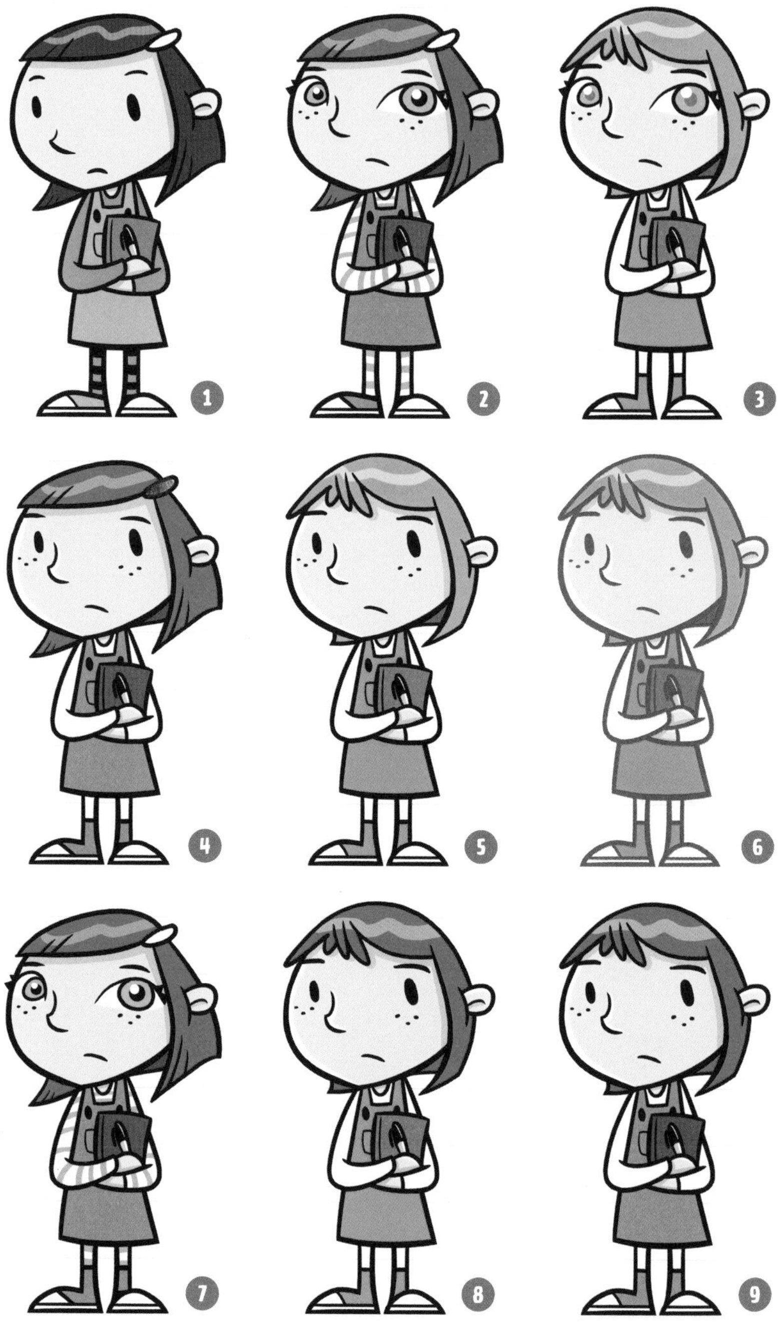
1
2
3
4
5
6
7
8
9

Answer: Number 4!

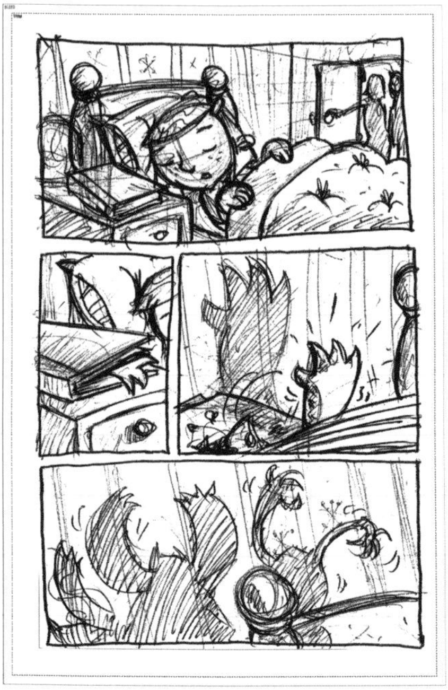

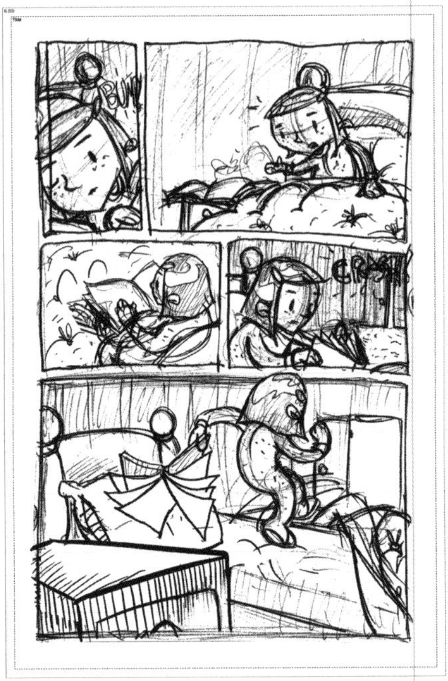

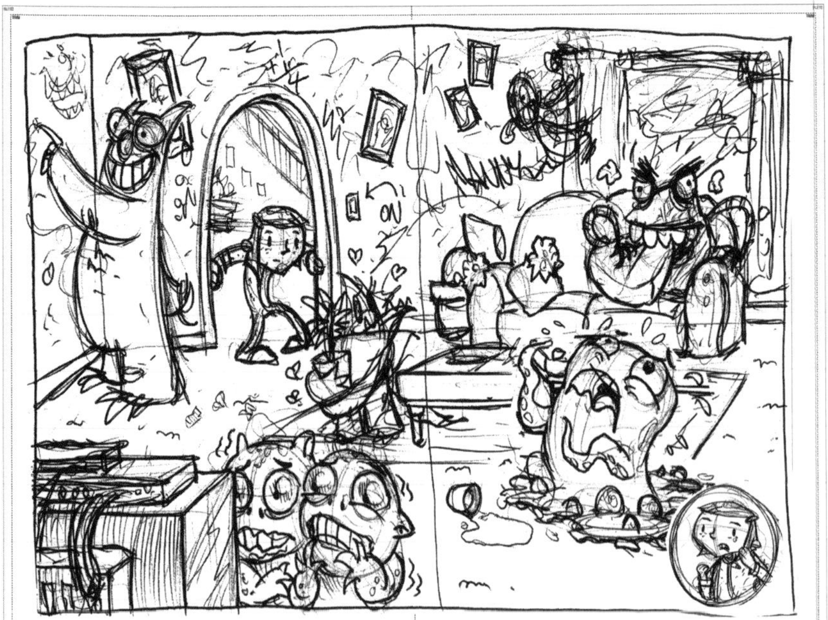
ON

Here's how the pages look once Vinny's drawn each page in pen.

ABOUT THE AUTHORS

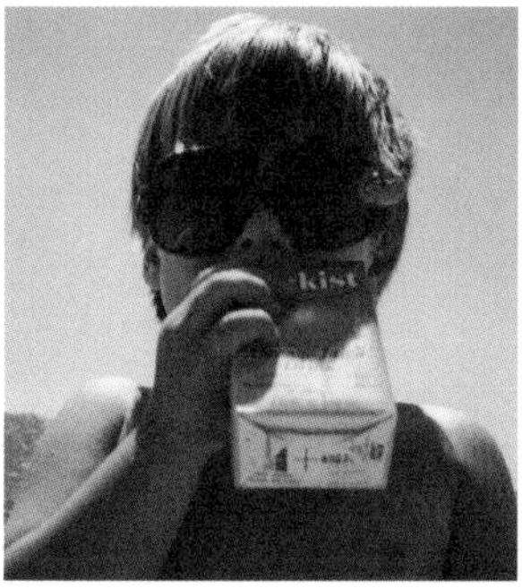
kist

www.thejoshuawilliamson.com

JOSHUA WILLIAMSON resides in Portland, OR, where he writes comics and kids books while living with his awesome wife, Danielle, and his loyal dog sidekick, Cordelia. He has written for a wide variety of publishers. Sketch Monsters marks his fourth book with Dear Dracula collaborator Vicente "Vinny" Navarrete. Josh writes comics for a living because he can't sing or dance or hit a free throw.

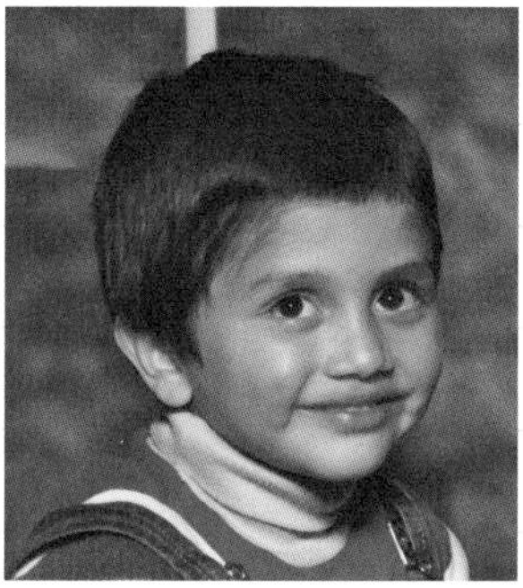

www.vinnyville.carbonmade.com

VICENTE "VINNY" NAVARRETE is an Oregon born artist who, when not drawing, spends his time playing basketball, reading comics, and eating cheese.

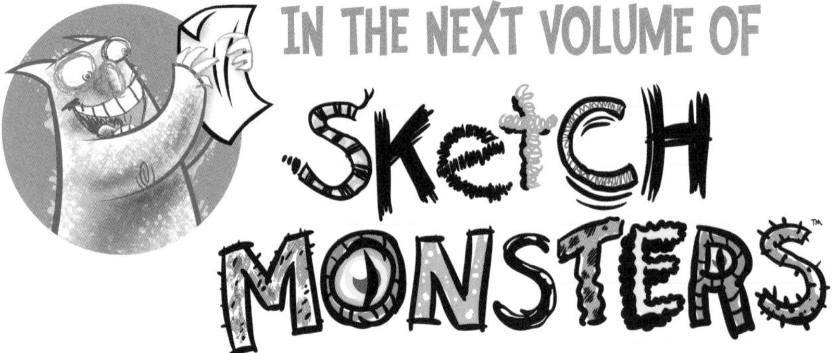

IN THE NEXT VOLUME OF SKETCH MONSTERS™

Mandy and her monsters learn that she isn't the only artist with a magic sketchbook!

MORE FUN COMICS FROM ONI PRESS!

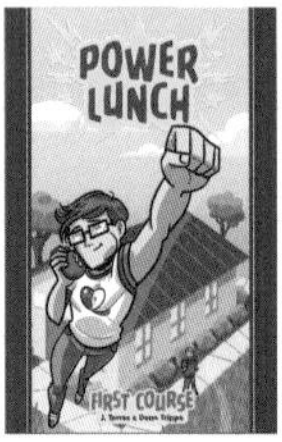
POWER LUNCH
FIRST COURSE

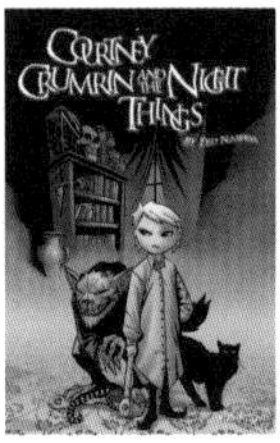
COURTNEY CRUMRIN AND THE NIGHT THINGS

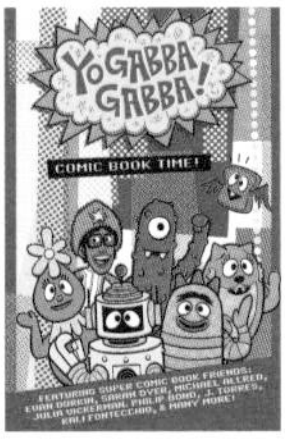
YO GABBA GABBA!
COMIC BOOK TIME!

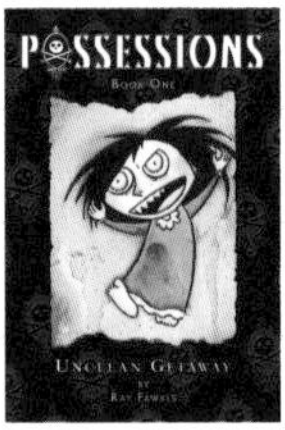
POSSESSIONS
BOOK ONE
UNCLEAN GETAWAY

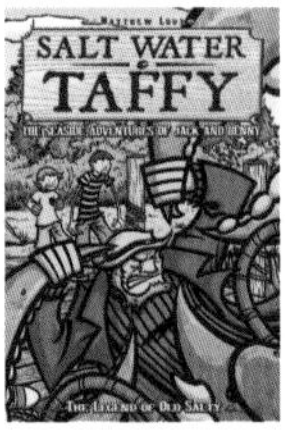
SALT WATER TAFFY
THE LEGEND OF OLD SALTY

POWER LUNCH - VOLUME 1: FIRST COURSE

By J. Torres & Dean Trippe

40 pages • Color • $12.99 US • 978-1-934964-70-5

COURTNEY CRUMRIN - VOLUME 1: THE NIGHT THINGS

By Ted Naifeh

128 pages • Digest • Black and White •$11.95 US • ISBN 978-1-929998-60-9

YO GABBA GABBA! COMIC BOOK TIME! VOLUME 1

By Evan Dorkin, Sarah Dyer, Michael Allred, Julia Vickerman, Philip Bond, J. Torres, Kali Fontecchio, and more!

128 pages • Hardcover • Color • $24.99 US • ISBN 978-1-934964-49-1

POSSESSIONS - VOLUME 1: UNCLEAN GETAWAY

By Ray Fawkes

88 pages • Digest • Black, Green, and White • $5.99 US • ISBN 978-1-934-964-36-1

SALT WATER TAFFY - VOLUME 1: THE LEGEND OF OLD SALTY

By Matthew Loux

96 pages • Digest • Black and White • $5.95 US • ISBN 978-1-932664-94-2

For more information on these and other fine Oni Press comic books and graphic novels, visit www.onipress.com. To find a comic specialty store in your area, call 1-888-COMICBOOK or visit www.comicshops.us.

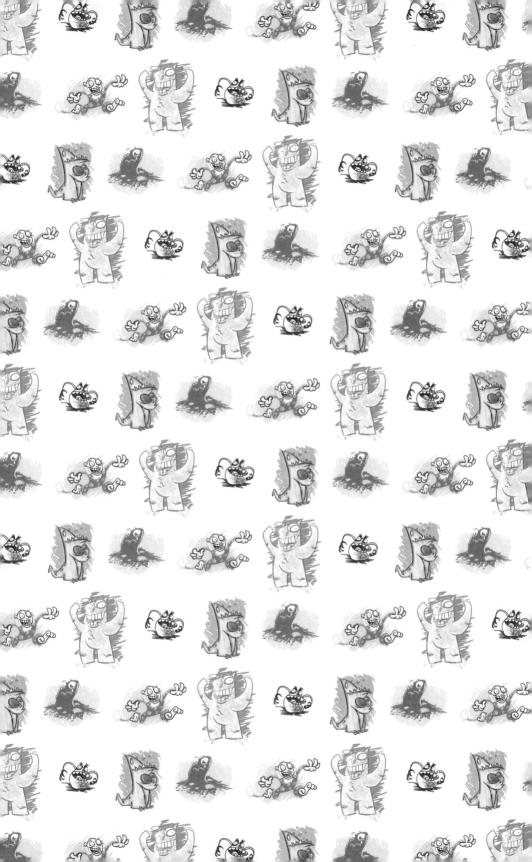

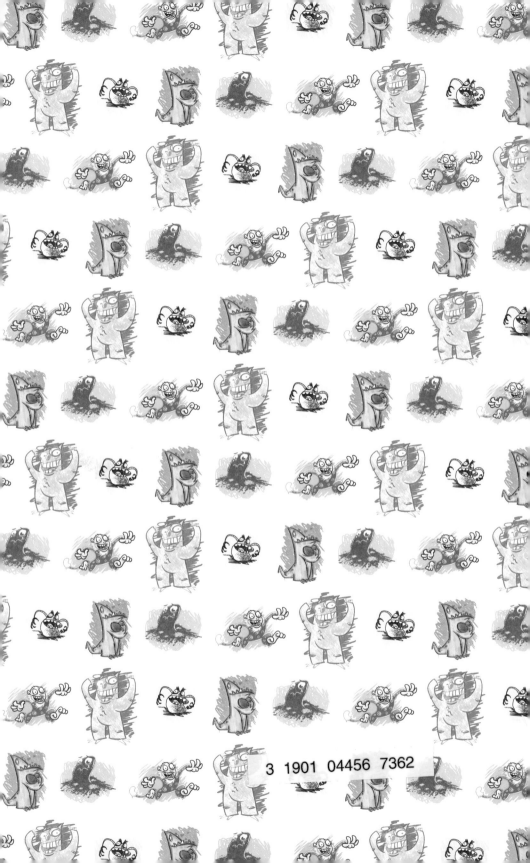